POSTCARD HISTORY SERIES

Decatur

This is the earliest known postal card mailed from Decatur, Alabama, on May 16, 1874, requesting a "catalog of practical and scientific books" from Philadelphia, Pennsylvania, to be sent to Trinity Station in Morgan County for pickup. This is also one of the earliest government postal cards, known to collectors as a GPC, with a four-bar post cancel. The term postal card differentiates it from a postcard, which is a term to designate cards prepared by private companies and which do not have prepaid franking. (Author's collection.)

On the Front Cover: Bank Street is pictured looking north from Vine Street in Decatur. The card was mailed from Decatur on June 16, 1924, from F.W. to Miss Mary Dunn of Newberry, South Carolina. According to census records, she was born in 1897. F.W. was possibly a railroad engineer, as he wrote, "I am running between Birmingham and this place [Decatur] now. I like this run better. Hope you found everybody well when you got home." The card is a divided back chromolithograph produced by the E.C. Kropp Company of Milwaukee. (Author's collection.)

On the Back Cover: This card shows moonlight on the Tennessee River in New Decatur, Alabama. It is a depiction of the area of the river on the southeast side of what at the time was a separate city founded by northerners after the Civil War. The town changed its name from New Decatur to Albany in 1916. It would be some 10 years later before Albany finally joined with Decatur to form one town. The card is a divided back chromolithograph mailed November 3, 1912, from New Decatur to Miss Ola Myers in Hamilton, Ohio. It reads, "Hello all, How are you getting along? We are all well except bad colds and they are plentiful." (Author's collection.)

POSTCARD HISTORY SERIES

Decatur

Jonathan Ford Baggs

ARCADIA
PUBLISHING

ISBN 978-1-4671-0294-0

Published by Arcadia Publishing
Charleston, South Carolina

Printed in the United States of America

Library of Congress Control Number: 2018953572

For all general information contact Arcadia Publishing at:
Telephone 843-853-2070
Fax 843-853-0044
E-mail sales@arcadiapublishing.com
For customer service and orders:
Toll-Free 1-888-313-2665

Visit us on the Internet at www.arcadiapublishing.com

This book is dedicated to past, present, and future residents of Decatur, Alabama. Especially to my parents, my son, my brothers, and my sister.

Contents

Acknowledgments		6
Introduction		7
1.	The Downtowns	9
2.	Boardinghouses, Motor Courts, Motels, and Hotels	25
3.	A Bridge, a Dam, and Something to Eat	51
4.	Steamboats and Cotton	63
5.	The Railroads, Boom to Bust	75
6.	The Old State Bank	87
7.	Views of the Decaturs	91

ACKNOWLEDGMENTS

I would be remiss to not include all who have encouraged me in the fields of writing and historical research, for they made this work possible either directly or indirectly. Sadly, some are gone but their inspiration was immeasurable. Suzanne Lacy and Dr. William Foster both were outstanding educators who took time to encourage me in the pursuit of writing. John Caddell always had time for questions relating to Decatur. The staff at the Morgan County Archives, Libby Boggess and Mike Plemons, were most helpful. Thanks go to Dirck Losch for his help in translating some of the foreign-language cards and to Mary Roberts Morgan. Douglas Cubbison, as fine a historian as I've ever known, has always been a source of encouragement. Special thanks to Morgan County archivist John Allison and to David Breland, Decatur's director of historic resources, for reviewing the proofs. Also, thanks to Phyllis Roberts and Jennifer McNeese at the Decatur Public Library for their assistance. My title manager at Arcadia, Caitrin Cunningham, withstood countless tests of her patience, and her guidance was invaluable. Thanks go to acquisitions editor Erin L. Vosgien as well for her encouragement. I'm especially indebted to my mother and father for instilling perseverance in me—and also to my best friend, Boomer the Wonder Dog, for his unfailing love and affection before, during, and after the book's preparation.

For readers wanting a more in-depth examination of photography and printing processes related to postcard history and production techniques, Metropostcard.com, run by Alan Petrulis, is a go-to source of information and was a great help.

Every effort has been made to ensure the historical accuracy of this book. All images are from the collection of the author, except where noted.

Introduction

This book is not intended to be a time line history of Decatur. Rather, it is a look at how the city was perceived by residents and visitors during the eras illustrated here. A window into history can be found in even the most innocuous of things produced during a specific era. More than just a piece of cardstock for people to send quick messages at low cost, postcards reflect the influences of various art movements, advertising trends, changing societal views regarding the sexes and race, changing technologies and printing methods, and photographic advances—all intertwined into one object.

As it is, this book represents the most complete collection of postcards ever gathered in one place related to Decatur, Alabama. Some of the examples are the only known ones extant—assuredly there are some that have not been included due to scarcity or their own commonality.

Postcard collectors, or deltiologists as they are known, usually want pristine, unused postcards, but this book contains, for the most part, just the opposite. The majority of the postcards pictured here were mailed: sent to people expressing their hopes, desires, fears, and general disposition of themselves and the area in which they were traveling. Most were sent north, some were sent to Germany, Holland, Canada, and other points around the world. All carried a little bit of Decatur with them.

A word about handwriting. Since most of these cards were mailed to friends, family, and acquaintances, often a full name is not included but only a first name, and sometimes just "Grandpa," "Mother," or some such indicator of familiarity. Often, cards were sent in haste while traveling or catching a train. Some are in pencil or iron gall inks that have smudged over the last century, and handwriting itself is unique to each person. Punctuation has been added where lacking on the original cards for the convenience of the modern reader.

The city today really is a series of small communities on the banks of the Tennessee River that, over the decades, have become a part of the larger town called Decatur. A series of ferries were established here for crossing the river, with that of Dr. Henry Rhodes becoming the most prominent and giving the town its first name, Rhodes Ferry.

Decatur was organized in 1820, but it remained under the jurisdiction of the state as part of the Cherokee Reservation until incorporation in 1826. As the western terminus for downriver traffic, Decatur began to grow in importance as speculators eager for land in the rich valley flooded into the area.

One of the saddest tragedies witnessed by the fledgling town, although not seen as such at the time, was the final removal of the Cherokee and other Indian tribes, many of whom were forcibly disembarked from boats at Decatur to be shipped by rail to Tuscumbia, bypassing the dangerous low-water Muscle Shoals, and from there to faraway lands in the West, with scores dying along the way.

Residents of Decatur have also suffered, and sustained themselves, through serious tragedies and triumphs—financial collapse followed by war devastation, yellow fever epidemics, and more financial depression. Then the railroad shops saved the town. And once those shops closed, a series of mills took their place. Unwanted publicity was shined on Decatur and the South during the Scottsboro Boys trials, which set new legal precedents safeguarding rights to an impartial jury. During the heady days of the space race, the city was home to many NASA engineers, who would gather at tiny restaurants late at night to plot how to get a man to the moon and back.

It was US president Ulysses S. Grant, following the lead of other countries, who authorized postcards in this country in 1873. Printed on the back were the words "Postal Card" with a one-cent denomination. By law, only government-issued cards could use the words "Postal Card," and the postage side was only for use in addressing the card, with the message allowed only on the front. It wasn't until 1898 that the government gave up its monopoly on postcards. By 1905, collecting postcards had become a national craze and had turned into the world's largest hobby. The Kodak Brownie camera allowed anyone, from the general public and the local drugstore to large printing firms, to make their own real-photo cards. Decatur residents, merchants, and visitors alike joined in heartily sending cards back and forth the world over. This "golden age" of postcard collecting lasted roughly from 1907 to 1913. Families began to collect postcards for the images, and the focal point of the living room when entertaining during this era was the postcard album.

Decatur had several local businesses as well as amateurs producing postcards, and many of those are included in this book. Again, this book does not represent all of the postcards with a Decatur theme that were ever produced, but it does present the vast majority that historians know about.

Although the postcards here are grouped according to loose themes, several of them obviously overlap, whereas one that is labeled with the name of a bridge might also show a steamboat or some other point of interest. Some readers of this book may have never sent a postcard or even really seen one in common use. As such, the messages on the backs of some cards are presented so the reader can have a sense of their use and maybe try their own hand at deciphering sometimes century-old cursive writing, once the standard means of communication among people.

Today, the river flows past Decatur as always, an endless source of both exasperation and pride. The railroad tracks still send trains and commerce to and fro. Cotton is still grown. No city is perfect, and history is a cluttered pursuit with hidden truths behind each nugget of myth. Hopefully, readers will use the following vignettes and images as a starting point in their own pursuits of discovering just who we are and why we are here. And the river will keep flowing by, just as it did for those residents more than 100 years ago, just as it does today, and just as it will tomorrow. I hope you enjoy the journey.

One

The Downtowns

Decatur is unique in that it has two downtown districts tenuously connected together. Though today they are referred to singularly as "downtown," they weren't always viewed as such, but as districts belonging to two separate entities with their own post offices—the Second Avenue district of New Decatur/Albany and the Bank Street district of "Old" Decatur.

New Decatur was formed in 1887, primarily as a marketing ploy to attract northern investors to the area with promises of good land, water, rail transportation, and industrial prospects. New Decatur changed its name to Albany in 1916, to better reflect the primarily northern interests that had relocated here and to avoid the "Decatur" label.

Despite pleas and editorials for the towns to abandon their separate identities and join together, Albany held out before vacating its charter in 1923. In a symbolic show of unity, each town formed a parade: one beginning at Second Avenue marching north and one beginning at Bank Street marching south. The two groups met at the common boundary of Lee Street and ended their animosity by symbolically "burying the hatchet."

But it wasn't so simple as agreeing to unify. Taxes in Albany were higher, and that town had more debt, resulting in the Alabama Supreme Court declaring the junction of the two towns unconstitutional. These issues were not resolved until 1927, when the state legislature finally declared the two towns one city under the name of Decatur.

Postcards from this era bear postmarks of Decatur, New Decatur, Albany, and later New Albany, which by then was a substation of Decatur proper.

This real-photo postcard was sent from Decatur in March 1908 and shows a view of Bank Street's west side looking north from near Vine Street. In the far distance is the Old State Bank building. Most of the structures in the immediate foreground up to Lafayette Street still exist today. Structures past the Lafayette Street intersection and Church Street, in the middle distance, were torn down, with the exception of the Old State Bank. The card was sent to John Kavanaugh in Chattanooga, Tennessee, and reads, "Hello! Boy! How are you? Got your letter [yesterday]. Hope you will keep well now. Saw in [yesterday's] paper, Jimmie Sanders shot [name unintelligible] and it is thought he will die. This is my happy home. Paradise Alley! Go up at the bottom mark and roost on the second floor of left-hand building. Will write soon. Be good. Love from Annie." The writer made two black Xs on the card to indicate the entrance to her apartment and location of same. The card is a divided back, printed in Germany and published by Cartwright's Drug Store in Decatur.

A companion view to that on the previous page is this real-photo postcard of the east side of Bank Street from near Vine Street. While a few of the buildings still exist, those in the foreground have undergone significant structural changes. This would have been the immediate view of Annie from her apartment highlighted on the previous page. A confectionery's sign is easy to pick out along with two individuals dressed stylishly tending to the back of a General Merchandise wagon. A fresh pile of coal has just been delivered to the front sidewalk, while an individual in apron with shovel apparently is moving toward it. Under magnification, two young African Americans can be seen behind the men tending to the wagon. Another man, walking so rapidly that his image is a blur, can be seen with long coat and hat moving past the shingle for E.W. Godbey, Attorney at Law. Someone penciled in that the city had "about 10,000 population" and noted "July 1907." The card was published by the Souvenir Post Card Company of New York and printed in Germany.

This is a view of Bank Street looking south from Church Street. The Owl Drug Company, with its logo plainly visible, is on the left. Owl was founded in 1892 in San Francisco. The store was in business at this location from 1912 to the mid-1940s. The buildings on the left still exist, with some currently undergoing restoration. Buildings in the immediate foreground on the right no longer stand between Church and Lafayette Streets.

Focusing on the east side of Bank Street looking south and encompassing its intersection with Lafayette Street is this PCK image published by the Owl Drug Company. Of note is the construction of trolley car tracks, with the Williamson and Echols store at center. These buildings, for the most part, still exist. PCK stood for Paul C. Koeber Company, in business from 1900 through 1932, with offices in New York and Germany. Many PCK cards have a dark, heavy feel because of the thick layers of ink used in their processes.

With a view looking south on Bank Street is this companion image to those on the previous page that shows the west side buildings as an electrified trolley car enters from Church Street. Close inspection reveals a man hanging off the car at far right. Of note is the Star Theater. The buildings in the immediate foreground were razed during urban renewal in the 1970s.

This somewhat common card shows the Independent Order of Odd Fellows assembling on Bank Street at the Vine Street intersection. This particular branch of the fraternal organization was dedicated to the care of orphans, with a home established in Cullman in 1907. By 1923, the home had 97 children and cultivated 200 acres of farmland. The Great Depression took its toll though, and by 1938, the orphanage was closed. It was reopened in the late 1940s and today is known as Childhaven. The card itself is an un-posted halftone image, and the publisher is unknown.

Manufactured by the E.C. Kropp Company of Milwaukee, Wisconsin, this card is a chromolithograph of a real-photo similar to previous views of Bank Street, with a view looking north near its intersection with Vine Street. Brock & Spight Wholesale Grocers dominates the west side of the street, while McGhee Furniture is in the building on the east side where Bank intersects with Lafayette Street. The electric trolley line and track bisect the middle of the card topped with an early incandescent light bulb. This was a popular view at the time, as various companies published the same card utilizing a variety of ink processes. An identical card by the Rigo Chemical Company of Nashville, Tennessee, which, unfortunately would not reproduce accurately for this book, was sent to Mrs. John Poindexter of Detroit, Michigan, in mid-September 1910. The message reads, "My Dear Mrs. Poindexter, After a twenty-mile drive this morning I was very tired so I left the dinner table and landed in the hammock to take a nap when my thoughts wandered back to Detroit and settled on you. How are you anyway? Better I know [and] eating more fat meats and cabbage than they can cook for you. We are having a lovely time. Tomorrow we go to Huntsville to a collard fair. I went to church Sunday. Had lots of fun. George leaves today. I might stay until Oct. 1. Hoping you are much better. I remain your friend, Etta."

Captioned "Bank Street, Looking North," this card was sent from Decatur on October 15, 1940, to Mrs. Daisy Norris in Beloit, Ohio. In the middle left distance, where today an upscale restaurant does business, is a sign denoting a café. On the left is Nungester Drugs. This is a Curt Teich white border card from its American Art Colored series. The message reads, "Decatur, Tuesday P.M. Well we are still here. Bill had a bad night last night. Had one doctor [come] at midnight last night. Feeling better today. Much cooler here tonight. Want to leave here Thursday, Ollie." This image was popular on postcards. Another copy, sent from Betty Landers of 613 Third Avenue West in Decatur to Enon Valley, Pennsylvania, on June 9, 1945, reads, "Dear Mrs. Steel, Would like very much to exchange hobbies with you. If you will help me, what kind of china dogs [do] you prefer? I will gladly send one in exchange for either a pennant or miniature hat of Pennsylvania. Your Alabama friend, Betty Landers."

Although the card is labeled "2nd. Avenue, Decatur, Ala." and that is true today, at the time the photograph—and, indeed, the card itself—were made and later postmarked on September 13, 1907, this was downtown New Decatur, which was separate from Decatur. This section of Second Avenue shows buildings that largely remain today, with the Casa Grande Hotel dominating the left center of the block. Under magnification, this real-photo postcard shows individuals dressed in coats and the time as 8:20 a.m. A banner across the intersection at Johnston Street advertises the Rail Road Young Men's Christian Association (YMCA) Christmas Carnival. In the immediate right foreground is the intersection with Grant Street. Sent to Miss Theo Davis in Trinity, Alabama, the card's message reads, "Hello Theo, Have you decided where you are going to school yet [?] Wish you could come up here. I had such a nice time with you last week. Sarah Davis." This is another card by the Souvenir Post Card Company of New York and was printed in Germany.

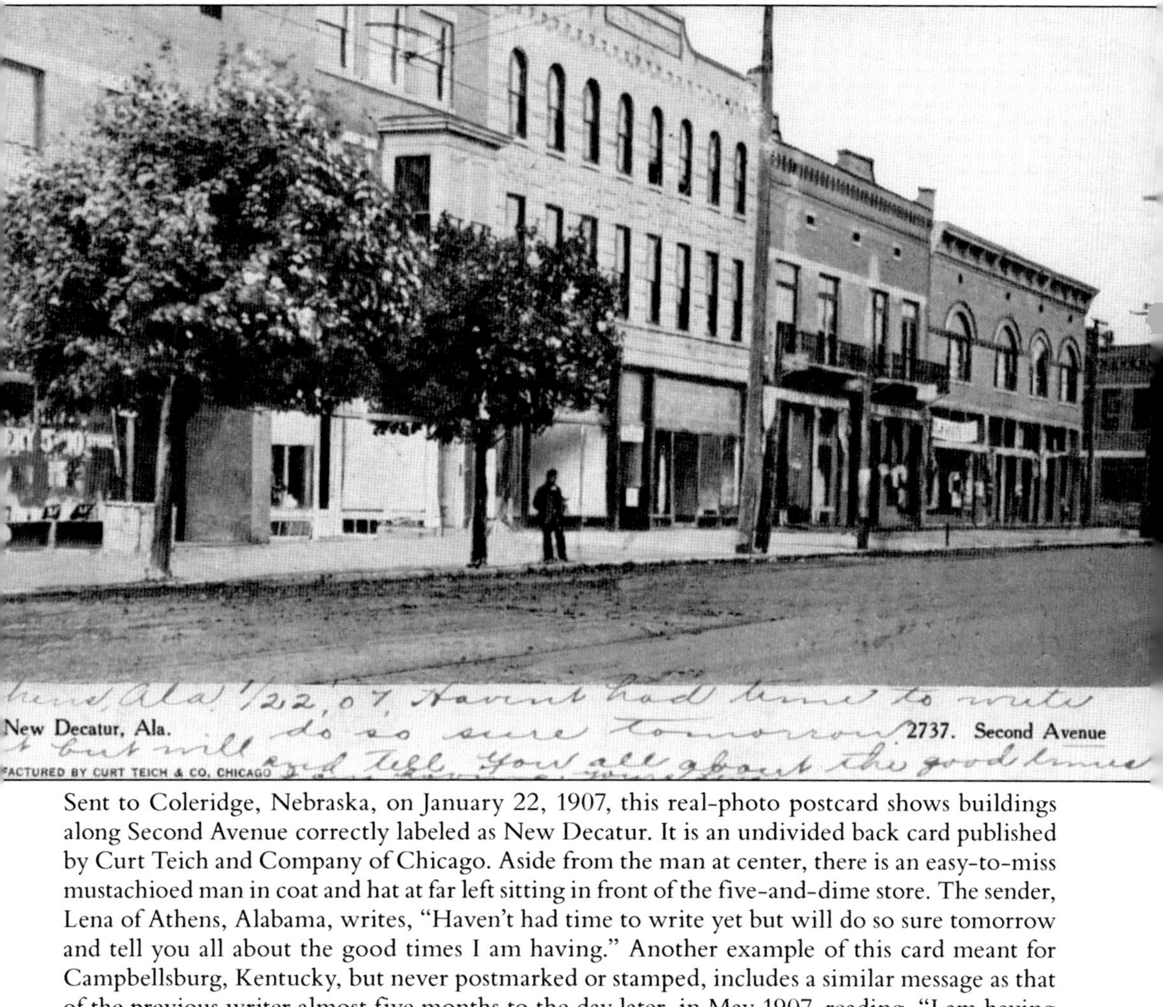

Sent to Coleridge, Nebraska, on January 22, 1907, this real-photo postcard shows buildings along Second Avenue correctly labeled as New Decatur. It is an undivided back card published by Curt Teich and Company of Chicago. Aside from the man at center, there is an easy-to-miss mustachioed man in coat and hat at far left sitting in front of the five-and-dime store. The sender, Lena of Athens, Alabama, writes, "Haven't had time to write yet but will do so sure tomorrow and tell you all about the good times I am having." Another example of this card meant for Campbellsburg, Kentucky, but never postmarked or stamped, includes a similar message as that of the previous writer almost five months to the day later, in May 1907, reading, "I am having a fine time in this place."

A lot of things are going on in the image on this card showing a good bit of the Second Avenue block between Grant Street on the immediate right and the intersection with Johnston Street in the middle distance. A one-dollar pocket watch is advertised in the window of T.H. Mattock's jewelry store. Farther down the sidewalk, what appears to be a shopkeeper has stepped outside in his shirt sleeves and is looking toward the photographer. At far left, the comic opera *Wang* is advertised with portraits of its star, matinee idol DeWolf Hopper. The show also featured the popular actress Della Fox. Set in Siam, Hopper played the country's regent, whose solution to his nation's bankruptcy is to marry a rich foreigner. It played in New York from May through October 1891 and enjoyed a revival in 1904. It gained immense popularity on tour around the country, thus an idea of the time frame of this image of New Decatur's Second Avenue can be ascertained to have been sometime in either 1904, 1905, or perhaps 1906. The building at far right remains today, while the large building in the middle right no longer stands. Sent from Decatur in November 1908 to Freehold, New Jersey, the real-photo card is a Curt Teich and Company product featuring an image tinted with a three-color process.

This is a closer view of the buildings that once graced Second Avenue's east side. Only the two at the end just before the intersection with Johnston Street remain. The card was postmarked in New Decatur on June 17, 1909, and sent to Henry W. Hildreth in San Diego, California. Its message reads, "Dear Henry, There is nothing new to tell. Business is awfully dull. Theo has come from Washington to pay us a visit. All are well, especially the baby. CPH." The card is a chromolithograph published by the American News Company of New York, Leipzig, Berlin, and Dresden.

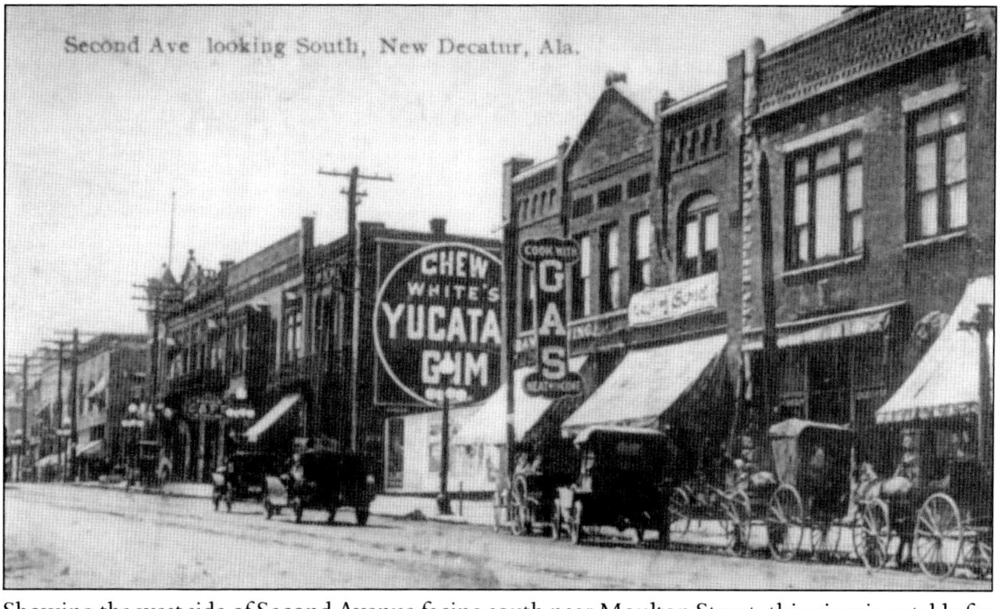

Showing the west side of Second Avenue facing south near Moulton Street, this view is notable for the large advertisement for White's Yucatan Gum. Also of note is the Palace Café at 511 Second Avenue. The large building at right with the stone-arch doorway was damaged during a storm in 2018 and demolished in 2019. This postcard is quite rare and was probably a product of the Souvenir Post Card Company of New York and printed in Germany. (Courtesy Decatur Public Library.)

Second Avenue is the most photographed street in Decatur, judging from the number of views published by different companies supplying postcards to the public. This view, a heavily colorized card from Curt Teich of Chicago as part of its American Art series, is notable for showing the locations of the Delite Theater in the middle left distance. And although the card is titled "Albany, Alabama," the post office sign above the left sidewalk reads "New Decatur." Sent on February 3, 1918, to Front Royal, Virginia, the missive on the card reads, "Dear Mrs. Jackson, Guess you thought we had forgotten you and all friends at post. I hope this will reach you well and running about fine by this time as you have has [sic] such a time. I like it here fine but I miss my home folks so much. Love all the Diddies for me. I remain yours, Mrs. Slaboda." The word "diddies" is unusual and can mean female breasts, little, or a fool. In the context of the message, it most likely meant "little," as in children.

This card showing yet another view of Second Avenue and is labeled "Albany, Ala." It was sent from that place on April 14, 1920. Over the years, what appears to be coffee was spilled on the back of the card, making the address illegible along with the name. The body of the note describes a flurry of activity in the Decatur area at the time including an early mention of airplanes, along with the death of the recipient's aunt and uncle. It reads, "Dear Lelana, do hope you are better. If this weather would get warm I know [it] would help you. Am sending you this card to show you our street cars in our town. Had an auto show and flying machines last week and a circus in town one day. I was afraid I would get run over. So much to look at. Your aunt and uncle were not separated very long. That is a nice way to go when people have lived together so long. Mother is not well and is coming back to stay with me. Much love, Neel."

During World War II, Decatur was home, albeit across the river at today's Pryor Field, to an Army Air Corps cadet pilot training center along with one in nearby Courtland. Servicemen and industrial workers came to Decatur, swelling its population. Sending a postcard was a quick and inexpensive way to stay in touch with family back home. This card, another Curt Teich product of Chicago and published by the Anderson News Company of Florence, Alabama, found its way into the hands of one of those who came to Decatur to serve the war effort. As seen in this view of Second Avenue looking north from close to the intersection with Gordon Drive, with Grant Street crossing in the middle distance, most of these buildings remain, though with some alterations over the years. Johnny sent the card to Cape Aircraft at Barnes Airport in Westfield, Massachusetts, on February 14, 1943. He wrote, "Dear Edie, Thanks for the 'cape news.' Am doing fine here. Am to start my own class of cadets off in two weeks. How goes the battle at cape [?] We did some flying in the snow here today. It reminded me of Westfield. 'Sunny South' phooey!"

This view of Second Avenue reflects change as Decatur's growth continued after World War II. Where once stood advertisements for a play some 50 years earlier at the Grant Street intersection, the W.T. Grant chain now has a department store, with Anderson Business College occupying the upper level. A young girl in a plaid poodle skirt is exiting Grant's, while another young lady with her back to the camera exhibits the fashion of the day. Goidel's Drugs was located just past J.C. Penney. Looking directly at the photographer in this real-photo image are two men on the corner, with one getting a shoeshine in front of the Emporium store and the shoeshine boy standing just behind his bent knee. Concrete street markers are in use next to the man with his hands in his pockets. The Princess Theater's marquee rises in the middle background. The postcard was published by the W.M. Cline Company of Chattanooga, Tennessee.

Postmarked from New Decatur on March 12, 1907, to Massillon, Ohio, this hard-to-find card shows Grant Street looking east from near Second Avenue. The Johnson Building, believed to be Decatur's first "skyscraper," at four stories, is at right. The top two stories burned a few decades later, but the building remains as one of the city's downtown anchors. Of note is the railing by the building leading to basement shops with a barely-visible arch of a basement window. Just as residents and visitors today complain about pollen in the spring, so too did the writer, noting, "It is warm and dusty here. My clothes were yellow this morning after taking a walk. Percy."

This real-photo postcard with a view closer to the Gordon Drive intersection looks north on Second Avenue. The color image shows a variety of shops and stores. Furniture, loans, shoes, appliances, novelties, and cafés populate the area, and modern traffic signals have been installed. This was the heyday of downtowns, before shopping malls eroded their popularity in the decades to come. Today, as the malls themselves are being shuttered, many communities hope to recapture this atmosphere. These buildings still exist, though some have undergone structural modifications. The card was published by the Alabama Post Card Company of Bessemer, Alabama.

Two

Boardinghouses, Motor Courts, Motels, and Hotels

Boardinghouses, motor courts, and hotels served travelers coming through or staying at Decatur as automobile use increased throughout the 20th century. Among these were the Hotel Echols, the Tavern, Speake's Tourist Rooms, the Cornelian Hotel, All State's Cottages (and Tourist Court), Hotel Lyons, the Pitts Motel, Magnolia Motel, and the Crescent Motel, among others. Postcards sent from these places served not only for communication purposes, but for adding to card collections at the time and as advertisements.

Cards were printed in great numbers, and pristine copies are readily available today. Harder to find are the ones that were actually used and sent through the mail. Early in the century, postcard collecting was a prime hobby, with clubs devoted to it around the country numbering in the thousands. Toward the middle and latter part of the 1900s, however, they were increasingly viewed as disposable and hence the scarcity of cards kept that made their way through the mail. Highly prized today are the real-photo postcards (RPPC) that show a realistic picture of some of these structures without the heavy use of colorization techniques.

Work on a new highway began in June 1912, on what was designated No. 31, which would run unimpeded from the Tennessee state line all the way to Mobile. It was known as "the Beeline Highway" because it was a direct route through the major cities at the time. North of Birmingham, it was referred to as the Decatur Highway, and south of Birmingham it was known as the Montgomery Highway. Although modern interstates today handle most of the traffic, US 31 still bisects Decatur and runs from Spanish Fort, Alabama, all the way to northern Michigan. For the bulk of the 20th century, US 31 brought travelers directly through Decatur. Hotels, motels, and tourist courts did a thriving business catering to the traveling public, and postcards served to put the area's best foot forward.

The Tavern Hotel in New Decatur, later Albany, was constructed in 1887–1888 on Grant Street at Sixth Avenue Southeast. One of the first buildings to showcase Decatur as a prime place for northern capitalists to invest, it was constructed on the highest point in the area, with a cupola offering expansive views of the burgeoning towns. With 125 guest rooms and a dining room accommodating 225, it played host to visiting dignitaries including Pres. Benjamin Harrison. Though it was called one of the most splendid hotels in the South, it lost money from the start, finally succumbing to the financial panic of 1893–1894, when it closed. Falling into disrepair,

it later operated as an apartment house, though postcards sent in the early 20th century indicate travelers still could find rooms here for the night. Advertised as fireproof when it opened, the Tavern burned in June 1923. The site of the hotel today is a parking lot. This is a real-photo postcard sent from New Decatur in November 1906 to Nashville, Tennessee, with a notation across the front reading "We are having a fine trip." This image would be the basis for many colorized postcards of the hotel.

This undivided back postcard of the Tavern, like many other images of the hotel, is based directly on the real-photo card seen on the previous page. Popular with railroad travelers, the hotel would send the wagon pictured here in front of the Grant Street facade to the New Decatur (later Albany) rail station. The station was at the foot of Grant Street in the area where the farmer's market is today. Passengers would ride to the Tavern, take their meal, and then be carried back to their waiting trains. The card is a Curt Teich of Chicago product sent to New Orleans from New Decatur. A message across the front reads, "July 25, 1907. Dear Miss Brooks, We left Mobile Monday and are in this place. Please write to me in care of this hotel. I phoned home since I came here. Mrs. Ewing." Another colorized card of this image was sent from New Decatur sometime between 1907 and 1916 to Mrs. Lillian Shelby of Waterloo, Alabama. The message reads, "Am so sorry I didn't get to see you again. And I did so want to meet your mother and Edwin and Temple! I guess I'll be seeing you when you go there on your way to Athens. Cassie Belle."

These two views of the Tavern show slightly different angles focusing more on the left facade, which faced what is today's Sixth Avenue Southeast. Though official histories say the building was no longer serving as a hotel, the card above, postmarked March 11, 1913, indicates travelers could find at least a meal if not a room. Penning a note across the front, the writer tells a friend in Galveston, Texas, that it was cumbersome to have to dress formally for meals. A note on the back reads, "Just a card to say hello. I am having my second honeymoon. Will be here until the first of April and then go to Florida. Best love to Fred and BB. From your friend, Alice Phillips." The card is an E.C. Kropp divided back chromolithograph. The card below, dated from New Decatur on March 23, 1908, is an American News Company product. It was sent to Mrs. H. Cummings at 209 Arch Street in Meadville, Pennsylvania. The note reads, "Hello. I am still here. We expect to start back around the first. How are you all? I hope JC is still improving. Try and write me and Jaime before I leave here if you can. 316 Jackson Street. Mary."

Hotel Lyons, Decatur, Ala
YONS

As the Tavern was in decline in neighboring New Decatur/Albany, the Hotel Lyons on Bank Street was in its ascendancy and renowned for its food service for decades. Standing on lower Bank Street at Walnut Street, it was a massive four-story structure across the street from the post office and a short walk from the Union Station at nearby Railroad and Vine Streets. The hotel was built in 1912 and opened for service April 1, 1913. Multiple postcard views of the building show that between 1923 and 1928, the hotel was enlarged to encompass most of the entire block on Bank Street. It remained in business for decades before falling victim to urban renewal and was torn down in 1971. The postcard is a real-photo card that bears the hallmarks of being a locally produced product, though it was never mailed. Quite an early image of the hotel, it shows the building before it was expanded and predates 1928.

The above card showing the Hotel Lyons is a real-photo postcard produced with the chromolithograph three-color process and is stamped "photo by Kirby." The Kirby Studio was at 222 Grant Street, according to the 1913 classified business directory. The card below was sent from Decatur in June 1923 and is an early and elaborate white-border card showing the hotel before expansion with somewhat fanciful Victorian dress on the painted-in individuals, which was out of style by the time the hotel was built. It was produced by the E.C. Kropp Company of Milwaukee. The card was sent from Decatur to Mrs. Annie Todd in Baltimore, Maryland. It reads, "Dear Mrs. Todd, How are you by this time? Claude got his leg broken four weeks ago. He is not able to get out of bed yet. John and Ora have the measles. Write to me sometime Mrs. Todd. I would like to hear from you. Your friend, Mrs. Chenault."

Expansion of the Hotel Lyons is evident in this image, along with tag lines used to entice interest in the area,"Upper Muscle Shoals City" and "the Gateway to Alabama." A Curt Teich and Company of Chicago product, the card was sent to St. Louis, Missouri, in March 1936, with a missive reading, "Sunday night 7:30. On our way home. Over night here. All tired out. Mom."

Sent to Wichita, Kansas, in January 1941, this Hotel Lyons card advertises "the South's Best Inland Fishing." Sent to Mrs. Harry Crandell, it reads, "Dearest, I'm working hard and making good but too tired to write. Leave in a.m. for Montgomery, Alabama, for a week. Then on to Florida. It's warm here and lovely. Been raining too. We've been here a week. Four of us. And we do have fun. All doing fine and making money too. I meant to write sooner. Will too. Love always, Carl." It was manufactured by Mid-West Map Company of Aurora, Missouri.

The Hotel Echols stood on Bank Street at Vine Street, just a short block up from the Hotel Lyons. This real-photo postcard was mailed from Decatur on May 27, 1912, to Mrs. Alta Roth in Philadelphia, Pennsylvania. It reads, "Dear Alta, Many thanks for your kindness. Hope your glasses will be satisfactory. Hope you are all well and having a fine time. How are your Sunday school babies? Also, the Curtis Publishing Company? With love to you all." The signature is illegible, and the card's publisher is unknown. Of particular note in this image is the distant view looking down Vine Street toward the railroad. The Curtis Publishing Company was founded in Philadelphia in 1891 and became one of the largest and most influential publishers in the country during the early 20th century. Its publications included *The Ladies' Home Journal* and *The Saturday Evening Post.*

Another real-photo postcard of the Hotel Echols shows its expansion and an individual perched in a third-floor window looking at the photographer. This is a white border card, which indicates a publishing date of sometime in or after 1913. Of note are the telephone lines just outside the third-floor windows on the corner. It was one of these lines that saved the life of hotel manager J.L. Harris when the building caught fire in February 1928. A newspaper account states that Harris hurried to the third floor to help guests get out of the burning hotel. He became trapped by smoke and flame and jumped from the window, "grabbing a telephone line and swung from it to the ground." Harris was not severely injured, suffering some hand lacerations from his high-wire escape. Five other people were injured in the blaze, and though it was vowed the hotel would be rebuilt, apparently the fire marked its demise. A structure that once was a hospital now occupies the spot on Bank Street.

Another white-border card with double postmarks was apparently sent through the mail twice—once in 1915, and again from Albany, Alabama, in June 1926 to Mr. and Mrs. A. Tanner in Saginaw, Michigan. The message on the back reads, "June 6, 1926, Dear Ames, Suppose you will be surprised to hear from us here, but came here Thursday as Robert took sick in Birmingham Monday 31st of May and had doctor two times there. His stomach again. Herbert and Maude came and brought us back here Thursday. We thought it would be quieter here as it was so noisy there. Robert is fine today and as lively as ever. Wouldn't even know he'd been sick. Ate good too. Will write more later. Love to all, Esther." The card is a colorized chromolithograph published by the Knoxville Engraving Company of Knoxville, Tennessee. Note that the hotel's second-floor balcony has disappeared in this image compared to previous cards featuring the Echols.

The Cornelian Hotel fronted Sixth Avenue at Johnston Street. It was established by E.C. Payne, mayor of New Decatur, at the turn of the 20th century and was contemporary with both the Echols and Lyons Hotels and was just a block from the famous Tavern Hotel. This popular postcard is easy to find today, with the bulk being linen cards from the 1940s. Sunday after-church dinners in the hotel's dining room were a regular event for Decatur citizens, and visitors and many civic clubs met there as well. The hotel's third floor hosted jurors in a notorious murder trial in 1945. Three years earlier, a man who would be known worldwide in the decade to come spent his honeymoon in the hotel. His name was Sam Phillips, and he signed a young Elvis Presley to a recording contract and changed the world of music forever. After the hotel's heyday, it was torn down in 1973.

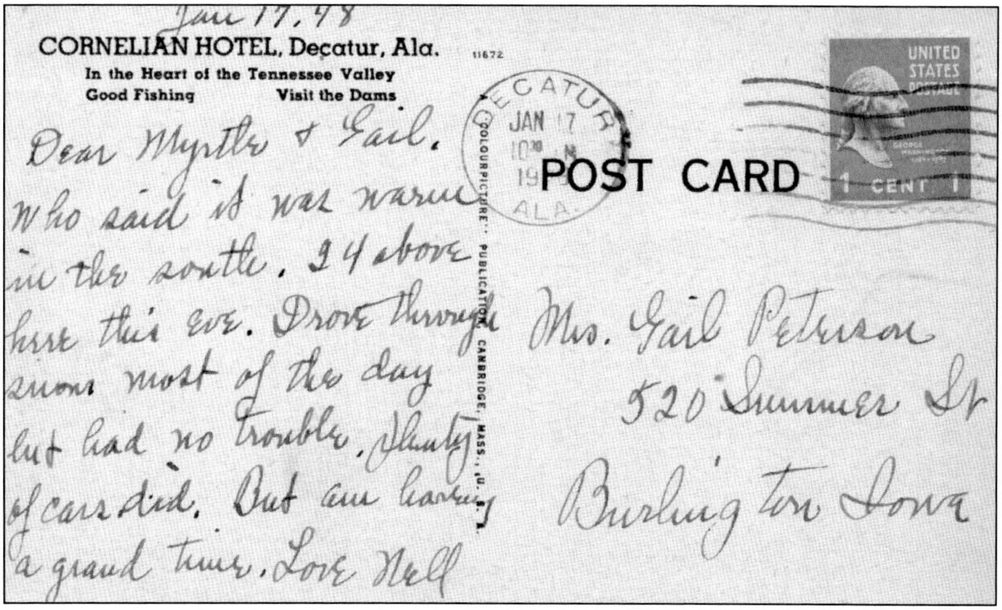

This is an example of the backs of Cornelian Hotel cards with "Good fishing" and "Visit the Dams" as tag lines. This is a card sent January 17, 1948, to Mrs. Gail Peterson in Burlington, Iowa. It reads, "Dear Myrtle and Gail. Who said it was warm in the south[?] 24 above here this eve. Drove through snow most of the day but had no troubles. Plenty of cars died. But are having a grand time. Love, Nell."

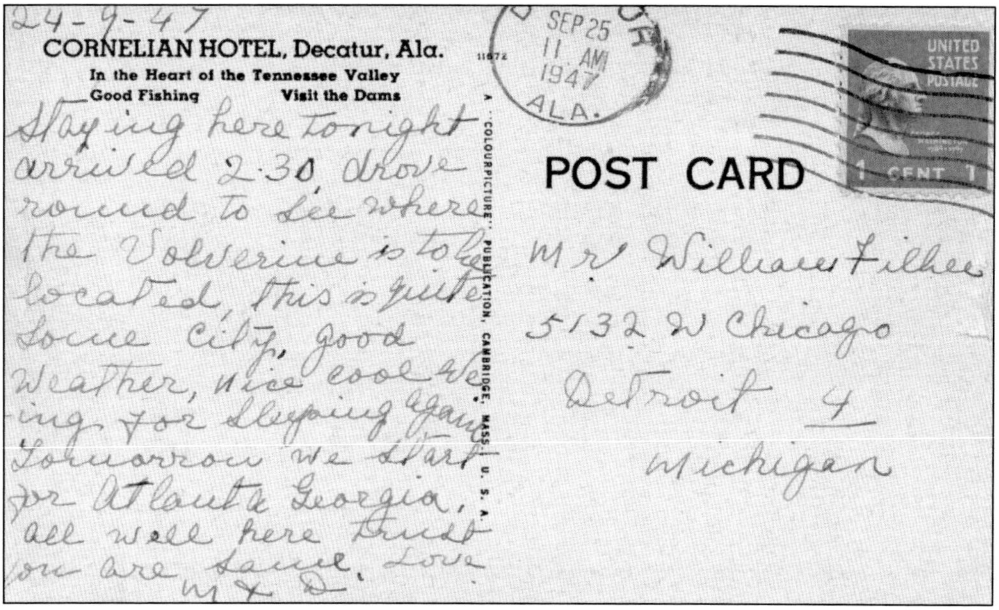

On this card sent to Detroit, Michigan, on September 25, 1947, these travelers wrote, "Staying here tonight. Arrived 2:30. Drove round to see where the Wolverine is to be located. This is quite some city. Good weather, nice cool evening for sleeping again. Tomorrow we start for Atlanta, Georgia. All well here. Trust you are same. Love, M &D." The Wolverine Tube plant began construction in 1946 on the banks of the riverfront and became one of Decatur's largest employers. In 1948, it shipped the first copper tubing produced in the South.

CORNELIAN COURT APARTMENTS — DECATUR, ALA.

Cornelian Court Apartments were built alongside and south of the Cornelian Hotel facing Sixth Avenue as well as behind the hotel and facing Grant Street. Sixteen apartments, each containing four or five rooms and separated by a 50-foot courtyard between buildings, opened in April 1928. "A desirable home for desirable tenants" was the advertising tagline. This postcard is another Curt Teich of Chicago product with serrated edges and full color. Sent to Chicago, Illinois, on December 23, 1937, the message reads, "From the looks of this card you will know we have started home. Hope to be there for Christmas if everything goes OK. We are coming home a different way so as not to miss anything. Marge and Jerry." The apartments remained viable, with several tenants living there for 20 years or more, before being torn down in the late 1980s. A chicken restaurant stands on the property today.

SPEAKE'S TOURIST ROOMS. 343 JOHNSTON STREET, SECOND DOOR WEST CORNELIAN HOTEL, DECATUR, ALABAMA C-6

The popularity of taking an automobile tour gave rise to a number of tourist courts and camps much like what today are called bed-and-breakfast establishments. One such place was Speake's Tourist Rooms on Johnston Street behind the Cornelian Hotel. This real-photo postcard shows the home complete with neon sign. The card was manufactured by the Fort Wayne Printing Company in Fort Wayne, Indiana. Although copies of this card occasionally can be found, none have been found that were actually sent through the mail. The home no longer exists, and its location is now a parking lot, although the house to the right still stands.

All States Tourist Court stood at various times just outside or inside the city limits of Decatur along the busy Beeline Highway (US 31 and today's Sixth Avenue Southeast). They included up to 48 cottages at peak operation between the 1930s and late 1960s. The cottages featured steam heat and "a popular priced coffee shop." This real-photo card was sent from Montgomery in November 1942 to Cleveland, Ohio. Though the postmark obscures part of the message, it reads, "Dear Sis and [illegible]. We are at Alabama with Don. He sure is fine. Love, Ford's Family." The publisher of the card is unknown. Today, the site of the tourist court is a U-Haul and mini-storage business on Sixth Avenue Southeast.

Kodachrome by Jack Taylor

All States Cottages, Highway U. S. 31

South of Decatur, Ala. (in City Limits)

This card was sent from Decatur on November 21, 1948, to Fort Wayne, Indiana. It reads, "Sunday night. Here is where we are tonight. Got cabins and supper here. I think we will be home Wednesday. We expect to get to Indiana Tuesday. We drove 400 miles today. Dad and Mother." By this time, the tourist court boasted porter service, "AA-1 Café, Fine Foods and Western Steaks and Southern Fried Chicken." An identical card was sent December 7, 1949, to Ontario, Canada. It reads, "Wednesday Noon. Well this is another beautiful day. We are having our dinner here. Sam has got his mits off today. It is just like spring. Men and boys in shirt sleeves. See a corn planter up the road. Don't know what they were planting but it look nice and straight. Cattle out in fields laying in sun. Everyone fine. Mom just read this and says it's OK."

Sent to Farina, Illinois, in February 1953, this card is a chromolithograph with a "Bursheen finish" published by the M.W.M. Company of Aurora, Missouri. It reads, "Dear Carole and all the family, We had a wonderful trip today. Stopped at 4 p.m. Now 5 and we had our supper. Have very fine cabins here at Decatur, Alabama. We all feel fine and had a fine time. Bye, Love Grandma." The old gabled roofs had disappeared from the units by this time, giving the cottages a more Art Deco appearance.

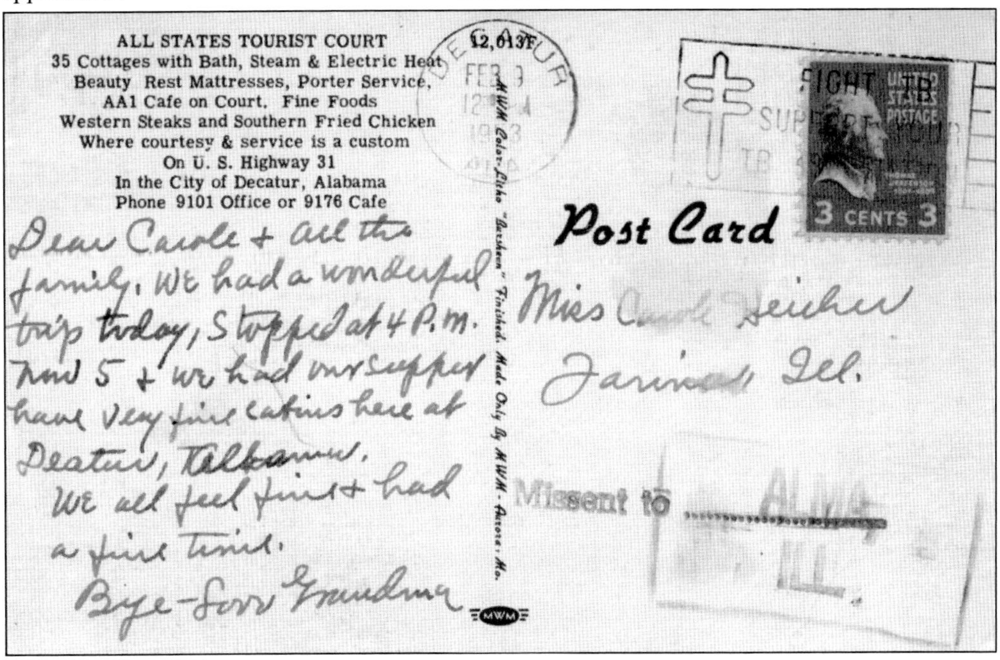

Motor and tourist courts reached their peak popularity in the 1930s through the 1950s. One that still exists today (without its famous magnolia tree) is the Magnolia Motel on Sixth Avenue Southeast. No mention of the motel occurs in local newspapers before 1956. As this real-photo postcard attests with classic automobiles in front, the motel's appearance has changed little, if any, since its construction decades ago. The card was published by the National Press of North Chicago and never mailed.

This is a glossy color, split, real-photo postcard of the Magnolia Motel published by the Alabama Post Card Company of Bessemer, Alabama, in the mid-1960s. It was mailed in 1965 to Huntington, Indiana, and reads, "We left home this a.m. at six o'clock. Had a little rain until almost Indianapolis, then cloudy all day. The sun finally shone about 4:45. Having a nice trip so far. Not much traffic. Best wishes, The Kases." During the 1960s, the Magnolia Motel served as a meeting place for some civic groups as well as a city election voting precinct.

Ushering in the era of modern hotel construction and aesthetics was the Downtowner Motor Inn on Johnston Street, directly across from where Speake's Tourist Rooms was located and across from the Cornelian Court Hotel also featured in this chapter. The Downtowner opened September 11, 1964, amid much fanfare. This is a real-photo color postcard published by Polychrome Picture Products of Decatur. It was sent to Cincinnati, Ohio, on December 18, 1970. By this time, the building was part of the Motel 6 chain. It remains in operation today at the same location and has undergone numerous name changes in the intervening years. The message on the card reads, "Had a grand time with you. Hope you make it down to Florida this winter. Rain part way, no snow. Ate and shopped in Louisville (oysters). Going to stay in Panama City Friday night. Taking our time. Evelyn and Tony."

Opened in early 1948 two miles south of Decatur's then city limits on US 31, the Pitts Motel featured 40 air-conditioned rooms with electric heat and a restaurant. By 1962, when it was sold, it had 52 rooms on 16 acres and was the third-largest in the area. Civic groups, bridge clubs, and industrial meetings all took place at the Pitts in the air-conditioned private dining room, which could hold up to 75 people. Remnants of the motel remain today under the American Inn brand. The card is unused and was published by MWM of Aurora, Missouri.

The Nite Fall Motel was another in a veritable explosion of motels south of Decatur during the 1940s and 1950s and opened next door to the Pitts Motel in 1955. The swimming pool was built of gunite and was host to many local children's swimming lessons. Still operating today under the Nite Fall Motel name, it bears little resemblance to its glory years, and the swimming pool has been filled in. Sent to Brookfield, Indiana, in June 1956, the message on the card above reads, "Dear Mother, I've just checked in here for the night (5:30 Monday evening) and hope to finish our trip tomorrow. There is only 30 miles from Cullman but we did not want to bother them. Love, Dorothy and Fred." The card was published by the Burnett Sales Company of Birmingham, Alabama. The card below is another Dexter Press of Nyack, New York, product published by Jim Cox, photographer, of 1515 Olive Street Southeast, Decatur. Never mailed, a message on the back reads, "Stayed overnight here, Aug. 31, 1962, on Florida trip."

As resort motels began coming of age, the Crescent Amusement Company of Nashville built its first commercial lodging enterprise a mile south of the Pitts and Nite Fall Motels on US 31. The Crescent Motel, built in 1960, was billed as "the South's most glamorous resort motel." Behind the motel and its restaurant was a golf course boasting play both night and day. It had two swimming pools, conference rooms, and a banquet hall. It also operated as a Ramada Inn and under various other names before it fell into disrepair and was demolished. Today, all that remains are two asphalt driveway entrances leading to an empty lot. Above is an artist's concept of the Crescent published by the Doyne Advertising Agency of Nashville. Sent to Columbus, Indiana, on October 3, 1961, it reads, "Sunday Eve. Hi Grandma. We are spending the nite here. First 400 miles from home, weather fine. Looks like rain, however lots of sightseers on the road today. Russ and Trey." Below is a real color photo of the motel sent to Saginaw, Michigan, on March 6, 1967, announcing the birth of an eight-pound baby boy.

If travelers continued south on US 31, about five miles away was the Deer Springs Tourist Court, featuring a restaurant and several cabins with carports. It operated throughout the 1940s until the early 1960s. Various newspaper ads in the 1940s cajoled area residents to visit an assortment of traveling psychics and palm readers who set up shop in the cabins among the traveling public. The above image is a real-photo postcard published by W.T. Cline of Chattanooga, Tennessee, and sent to Ohio in January 1948. Its message reads, "Hi everybody. Having a fine time. Are staying overnight at this court. Beautiful country, lovely roads and ideal weather. Alvin rode all afternoon in his shirt sleeves. Drove 199 miles today. 624 miles in all. Papa." Below is another real-photo postcard showing the cabins. Deer Springs was put up for sale in the early 1960s. In 1971, Deer Springs Baptist Church bought the property and built its sanctuary, where it remains today. All traces of the tourist court have long disappeared.

Wrapping up a look at Deer Springs Tourist Court are these two real-photo postcards. The card above shows the typical guest accommodations and was mailed December 27, 1947, to Gossville, New Hampshire. It reads, "Dear Mavis, We're on our way to Florida for a seven-day leave. Hope you had a nice Christmas with Ruth and Helen. Love to all, Earl B. and David P. [and] P and K." Showing the Deer Springs restaurant, the real-photo postcard below was mailed July 13, 1948, to Detroit, Michigan. It reads, "Hi Sis. Well we are on the way. Should get there Wednesday or Thursday. We are eating supper here. Notice glass top tables. By now. JS."

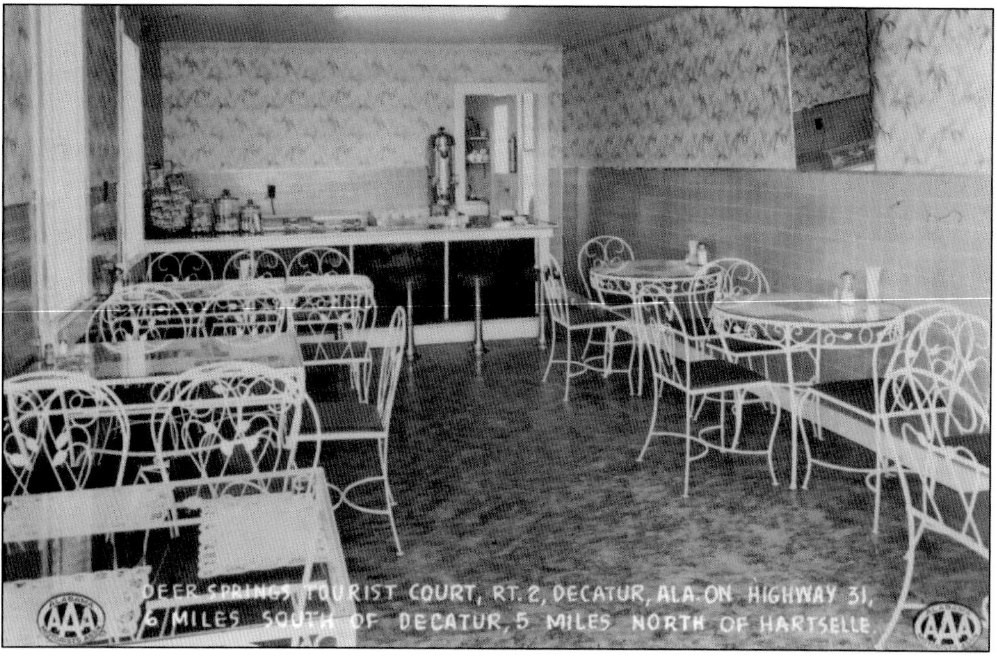

Three

A Bridge, a Dam, and Something to Eat

When the Tennessee Valley Authority built a series of dams to control flooding, aid commercial navigation, and mitigate infectious disease such as malaria, the structures became prime tourist attractions along with Keller Memorial Bridge. While going to see a bridge or a giant concrete dam may seem somewhat boring today, at the time they were seen as wonders of modern engineering. Not only did they fulfill their intended purposes, they also created a healthy tourism industry as a byproduct that served to advertise "the New South" to the country and world at large.

It was the building of Keller Memorial Bridge, and how to pay for it, that finally served to unite the two towns of Decatur and Albany. Until it was completed, the traveling public still relied on ferryboats to cross the river. The only bridge belonged to the Louisville & Nashville Railroad and Southern Railway. Named for Helen Keller's brother, William S. Keller, Alabama's first highway director, the bridge was completed in 1928. Decatur and Albany each put up $50,000 to help pay for it under the condition the state would pay it back. It would be a decade before the $100,000 was repaid to the then united town of Decatur. The bridge served the city until it was replaced in the late 1990s. Despite efforts to save a portion of it for pedestrian traffic, it was demolished in 1998.

When Congressman (and former/future general) Joe Wheeler first proposed a hydroelectric dam for Muscle Shoals in 1898, Congress managed to pass legislation for it and then promptly ignored it. In 1924, Wilson Dam was completed at Muscle Shoals. Still, there was debate, along with suspicious sentiments toward the federal project and the Tennessee Valley Authority. Wheeler Dam was green-lighted eventually and finally completed in 1936. Soon afterward, postcards of it began circulating through the mail sent by the traveling public.

A quite common and easy-to-find card today, this is a typical linen card of the era. New additives had been developed by the late 1920s enabling richer colors to be printed. But the new inks were thinner and would blur because they absorbed into the paper. Curt Teich came up with the idea of embossing his paper with a linen texture, which created more surface area, allowing inks to dry faster and allowing use of high-speed presses to produce them. This is a Curt Teich of Chicago product using the "colortone" process. Linen cards have the feel of art canvas and though they are based on real photographs, the paper's texture made rendering of sharp details difficult, so they were retouched and simplified, which was permissible with the growth of expressionism and abstraction in art circles at the time. Of note in this view from the opposite shore looking toward Decatur are the factories in the right background.

White border cards came of age after 1913, as the superior craftsmanship of German cards became more expensive to import just before World War I amid anti-German sentiment. These cards saved on ink and were better suited when being cut in sheets, as a miscut would only affect the border and not the image itself. They also required less skill than those produced by the German workforce. They took off in the 1920s and 1930s and could still be found for sale decades afterward. This card is another Curt Teich of Chicago product and shows the northern shore of the Tennessee River as viewed from Decatur. It was sent from Decatur on February 3, 1938, to Cincinnati, Ohio, and reads, "Drove 450 miles and arrived here 8 p.m. Cloudy skies all the way. Early April weather here. Temperature tonight 58. We are very tired. Clarence and Les."

The real-photo postcard above is a product of the Cline Photo Company of Chattanooga, Tennessee. Images of Wheeler Dam and all the various dams built by the TVA became the subject of postcards and were visited by the sightseeing public, who were curious to see such feats of engineering that provided cheap electricity and navigable waterways, and transformed the South. Locks allowing navigation of the Tennessee River are visible in the distance. The image below is also a Cline product showing the dam from the visitor's overlook, which is on the left above. Still a popular stopping point for those wanting to get a closer look at the facility, the overlook remains in use today.

Above is a card sent September 25, 1947, to Mrs. Bloodworth of 245 Clements Street in Paducah, Kentucky. Its message reads, "Hi Sweetheart, Just to let you know I am thinking of you. See you soon I hope. Haydon." The card is from the Curt Teich Company of Chicago's "colortone" series based on a photograph by G.W. Landrum. Another card from the same series is the image below showing the same location from the visitor's overlook as on the previous page. Sent from Decatur on Saturday, April 27, 1957, to Long Beach, California, the message on the card reads, "Greetings from the South! Have been here a week and expect to start for Dave's tomorrow. The 19-hour train ride was painful to back and left leg and Ruth's doctor found I had a bad disc condition which is going to curtail my activities. Overexertion in yard is . . . responsible for this setback. Lawson family is in fine shape and joins me in sending love to you and yours. Ethel."

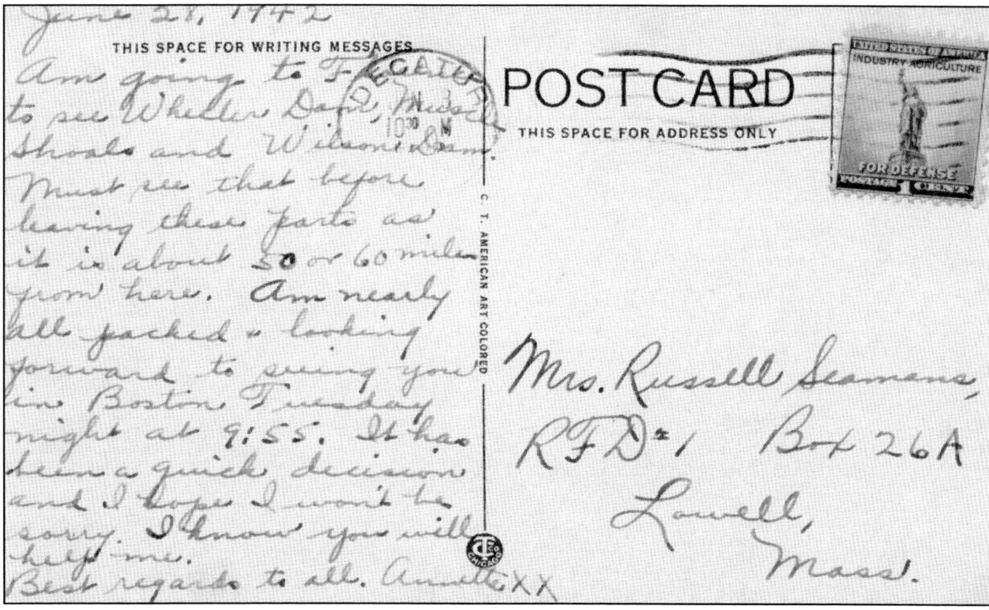

Here, a traveler looks forward to seeing the TVA dams. Sent from Decatur on June 28, 1942, to Lowell, Massachusetts, the card reads, "Am going to Florence to see Wheeler Dam, Muscle Shoals and Wilson Dam. . . . Am nearly all packed and looking forward to seeing you in Boston Tuesday night at 9:55. It has been a quick decision and I hope I won't be sorry. I know you will help me. Best regards to all. Annette."

A typical souvenir card from Curt Teich of Chicago reused old photographs and incorporated them into new artwork for tourists and collectors. This allowed the company to get more mileage out of previously used images. Each letter in "Decatur" is filled in with a previous postcard product—from left to right, Keller Bridge, Goodyear Tire and Rubber, Wheeler Dam, Decatur High School (known as "Riverside"), Central Baptist Church, Old State Bank, and the US Post Office on Bank Street. This card was sent to Alpine, Indiana, in January 1948.

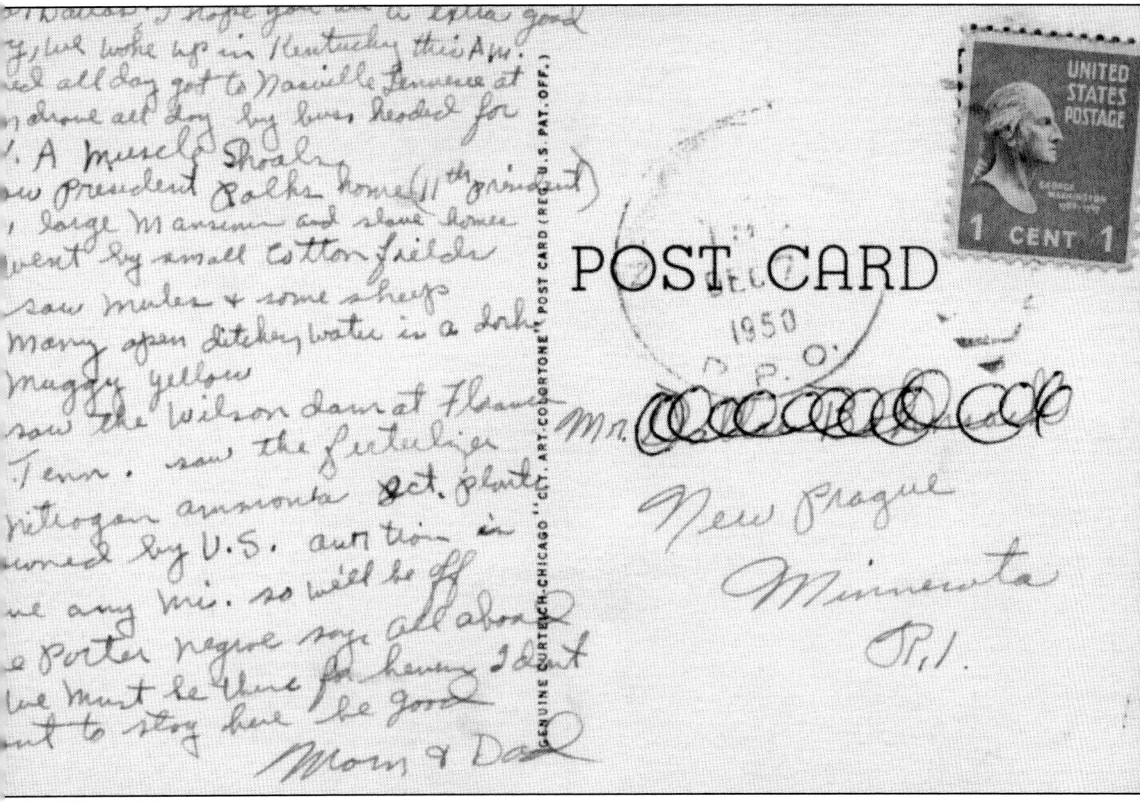

This is the back of a souvenir card identical to the one on the previous page and sent to New Prague, Minnesota, in December 1950. The writer mistakenly puts Florence, Alabama, in Tennessee. The note reads, "Dear Dallas. I hope you are a extra good boy. We woke up in Kentucky this a.m. Rained all day. Got to Nashville, Tennessee at noon. Drove all day by bus headed for TVA Muscle Shoals. Saw President Polk's home (11th President). Saw large mansion and slave homes. Went by small cotton fields. Saw mules and some sheep. Many open ditches. Water is a dark muggy yellow. Saw the Wilson Dam at Florence Tennessee. Saw the fertilizer, nitrogen, ammonia . . . plants owned by [the] U.S. Our train is due any [minute] so we'll be off. The porter negro says all aboard and we must be there for Henry. I don't want to stay here. Be good, Mom and Dad."

Greystone Cafe, at the River Bridge, Decatur, Ala.

Opened on December 13, 1945, at the foot of Keller Memorial Bridge, the Greystone Café and drive-in featured barbecued chicken, ribs, and seafood and steak for hungry travelers along the Beeline Highway. Its Maple Room upstairs hosted scores of private parties and banquets. It was painted "maple" and had green-tiled floors. No mention of the Greystone is found after 1959, when unpaid taxes of $18.75 were listed in litigation, and insolvency notices appeared in the newspaper. Posted from Decatur on January 30, 1950, to Cuyahoga Falls, Ohio, the note on the card reads, "We're all eating here at this place now. Wish you were here. Will get to Florida tomorrow or next day." The writer goes on to list her aunt's address, noting that it is one block from the beach. "We cater to tourists" is the restaurant's motto on the back of the card, a white-border chromolithograph published by Kaeser and Blair Incorporated of Cincinnati, Ohio.

Watkins & Perry Grill opened at 614 Sixth Avenue Southeast directly across from the Cornelian Hotel on Tuesday, September 16, 1946, serving steaks, chicken, and sandwiches "with a complete line of tobaccos and magazines." The restaurant also made note to "welcome all Alabama and Missouri football fans" that November for a special Thanksgiving dinner. It was operated by Harold Watkins and George L. Perry. No mention is made of the business in newspaper archives after December 28, 1950. In the 1960s, it was a steak restaurant, and for decades afterward the building served as Decatur Bait and Tackle Shop. The building still exists and was an office for a used-car lot, but currently is vacant The postcard was published by Shedd-Brown of Minneapolis, Minnesota, and was mailed from Decatur on June 5, 1954, to Hubbard, Texas. A message on the back reads, "Saturday. Well we are doing all the good. I am afraid I am going to gain though and [have to] let my dresses out. We are going to Culleoka [Tennessee] tomorrow and go to Ruby's Thursday and stay until we start home Monday. Love, Bess."

If travelers continued down Sixth Avenue (US 31 Beeline Highway), just before the city limits, they would pass Big Bob Gibson's Bar-B-Q restaurant. Presented here are two views of the business. Above is a real-photo postcard published by the National Press of West Chicago showing the restaurant as it appeared in the 1950s. The below view is the restaurant in the 1960s on a card published by the Vernon Company of Newton, Iowa. Gibson's restaurant was in business since 1925 at various locations along the Beeline Highway in Decatur; this was its prime location. In later years, it moved to a building next door and is still in business today and has become a city institution, winning awards nationwide and internationally for its food and sauces.

In early July 1959, on a narrow strip beside US 31 in Decatur, the Ce-Mar Restaurant opened for business next to Ryan's Gift Shop. In this view, the restaurant's sign is easy to miss on the far right of the card. Called a "View Gram" and published by Baxtone of Amarillo, Texas, this is a full-color glossy postcard advertising "sizzling steaks and chops" along with "fresh river catfish." Of note are the kitschy souvenirs advertised to entice travelers to stop. The restaurant and gift shop both were put up for auction in October 1965. A redecoration was completed the following April, in 1966, but mention of the business disappears afterward. Buildings remained on the property serving other business enterprises over the years since, notably an exotic pet store, but the Ce-Mar was no more and eventually all were demolished in the 1990s. The strip of land remains vacant today.

Harry Bell's Restaurant, "The Restaurant of Quality Foods," was farther south on US 31 and served seafood and steaks. Its private dining rooms, like those at other motels and restaurants, were available for receptions and civic group meetings. Not a lot of information is available on the business other than that the Girls' Club of Wolverine Tube held installation of new officers there in 1962. The restaurant may have been part of a chain, as several obituaries in Pennsylvania note the deceased once worked at restaurants with the same name in that state, but information is scarce. The card itself was published by Fort Scott Printing and Advertising of Fort Scott, Kansas, and is an uncommon postcard today. The building still exists virtually unchanged, though the surroundings no longer resemble the serene setting on the card, with multiple businesses nearby. Today, the building houses a longtime Italian restaurant named Alfonso's.

Four

Steamboats and Cotton

Decatur was incorporated in 1826, some six years after the town's designation and organization. Once land was open for development south of the Tennessee River and Decatur received its name and charter, a prime selling point was the rich soil ideally suited to cotton. Growing cotton was as close to growing money as one could get, provided one had the overhead, or the banking credit, to pay for land, seed, and labor, and then complete the task of getting it to market. If prices were high, growers could make a profit, pay off their loan, and repeat the process.

Getting the cotton to market was a major concern. Roads were rudimentary, where they existed at all. Decatur was situated on the south bank of the river, but the rocky shoals downstream meant using flatboats and keelboats, and even those were not always dependable.

Once in a while, a steamboat could navigate the shoals if the water was especially high. Solutions included building two canals, damming some of the creeks, and so on, but once built at costs of more than $600,000, the canals did not work as advertised and eventually were abandoned.

A permanent solution to unimpeded travel on the river didn't come until the Tennessee Valley Authority built a series of dams in the 1920s and 1930s. Until then, steamboat traffic was confined to the upper river from Knoxville to Decatur and the lower river route from Florence and points downstream; the routes were separated from each other by the rocky shoals. It was considered quite daring and risky for a boat captain to attempt navigating between Decatur and Florence; those who did, and survived with their boats intact, were feted as celebrities.

Cotton was thought to be harsh on soil and was said to "wear it out." The crop needs nutrients like sulfur, zinc, and phosphorus potassium. Irrigating cotton fields where the crop is rotated every three or four years was not common practice. With vast amounts of money to be made, growers couldn't resist. But growing only one type of crop in a field can lead to a deficiency in nutrients and lower resistance to soil diseases and pests.

Needed too were people to pick the cotton. Before the advent of machines and after slave emancipation, African-Americans and poor whites still worked the fields in backbreaking manual labor as sharecroppers. With money on the line that would be needed to survive until next year's crop was harvested, getting the cotton off the fields and transported to market meant days in the field picking from morning till dusk. Some picking would even go on through the night, such was the thin line between bankruptcy and survival.

Sent to Holland from Decatur on December 26, 1907, this card is an early divided back real-photo postcard produced in Germany and published by the Souvenir Post Card Company of New York. The writing in Dutch on the upper right translates to "cotton bales here off to market." At the time, a swing span was the only bridge across the Tennessee River. The boat is a flat barge with shallow draft for negotiating the rocky shoals downriver some miles to the left of the scene pictured. Received on January 10, 1908, in Holland, the card took two weeks to travel from Decatur across the ocean, where it remained for 100 years and through two world wars before making its way back to the city from whence it was sent.

Another real-photo postcard shows bales of cotton being loaded at the foot of Bank Street. The *Decatur No. 1* steamboat on the right was one of the last to be operated at Decatur before being scrapped in the 1930s. The other is the *John A. Patten* (sometimes misspelled as "Patton"), built in Jefferson, Indiana, in 1906, and burned at Bridgeport, Alabama, in 1910. It was the *John A. Patten* that was involved in a race in February 1907 with a towboat called the *Parker*, which blew up nine miles downriver from Chattanooga killing three crew members and leaving the *John A. Patten* as victor. In the photograph, several African Americans are engaged in securing bales of cotton or taking a short rest from their labors. On board the *John A. Patten* is a woman in formal dress with a similarly dressed man beside her. The card was sent from Decatur on June 12, 1909, to Balko, Oklahoma. Produced in Germany and published by A.M. Simon of New York, the card carries the message, "Dear Bro, we arrived here this morning about 8:30 a.m. Having a grand time. I'll write later. Bess."

The heavily retouched color postcard above, from the E.C. Kropp Company of Milwaukee, shows the John A. Patten steamboat docked at lower Bank Street. Sent from Decatur on September 11, 1911, by Professor Orsory to the International Harvester Company in Milwaukee, its message reads, "My best regards from here. I have good journey. Tomorrow I go a Moulton." By this time, the *John A. Patten* had burned and been scrapped. An identical card was sent from New Decatur on February 15, 1910, to Nevada, Ohio, and contains a simple message: "Greetings from the sunny South." The image below is another American News Company of New York and Germany chromolithograph of a real photo showing cotton loaded on a flat-bottom barge. Sent from New Decatur on February 17, 1908, to Oil City, Pennsylvania, the message reads, "Hello everybody. Tell mama I will write to her in a few days. By Aunt Mary."

Compress Yards, showing 26,000 Bales of Cotton, Decatur, Ala.

The fascinating real-photo image on this card shows a silhouette of the 1892 Morgan County Courthouse, which burned in 1926, in the right background as seen from the yards of the Southern Cotton Compress across the railroad at Moulton Street. Smoke from a steam engine rises in the right center while workers tend to the cotton bales. The card was sent from Decatur on May 19, 1908, to Northfield, Vermont.

This is another view of the Southern Cotton Compress yards at New Decatur. No publisher is evident on the real-photo postcard. The facility is still in business today at the same location under the name Union Compress and provides warehouse facilities, particularly to the cotton industry.

E.C. Kropp of Milwaukee published this chromolithograph of the cotton compress yards based on an image by the Decatur Kirby Photography Studio. It was sent from New Decatur on December 12, 1910, to Pensacola, Florida. The message reads, "Yes I remember and was going to send a card before this. Am having a bad attack of tonsillitis and my uncle is having grippe [diarrhea and stomach cramps]. I wish we were back in Ohio. It is so damp here. I don't like it as well as at home. Guess I'm homesick. Would be glad to start back tomorrow. I hope you are having a better time than us. Sincerely, Mildred Baird."

Sent without a message to Harrisonburg, Virginia, on October 4, 1909, most probably to a collector, this is a colorized card of the Cotton Compress yards showing the bales lined up ready for transport by railcar. Images such as this were important in advertising the rich opportunities for manufacturers to locate in the Decatur area. No publisher is evident on the card, which was printed in Germany.

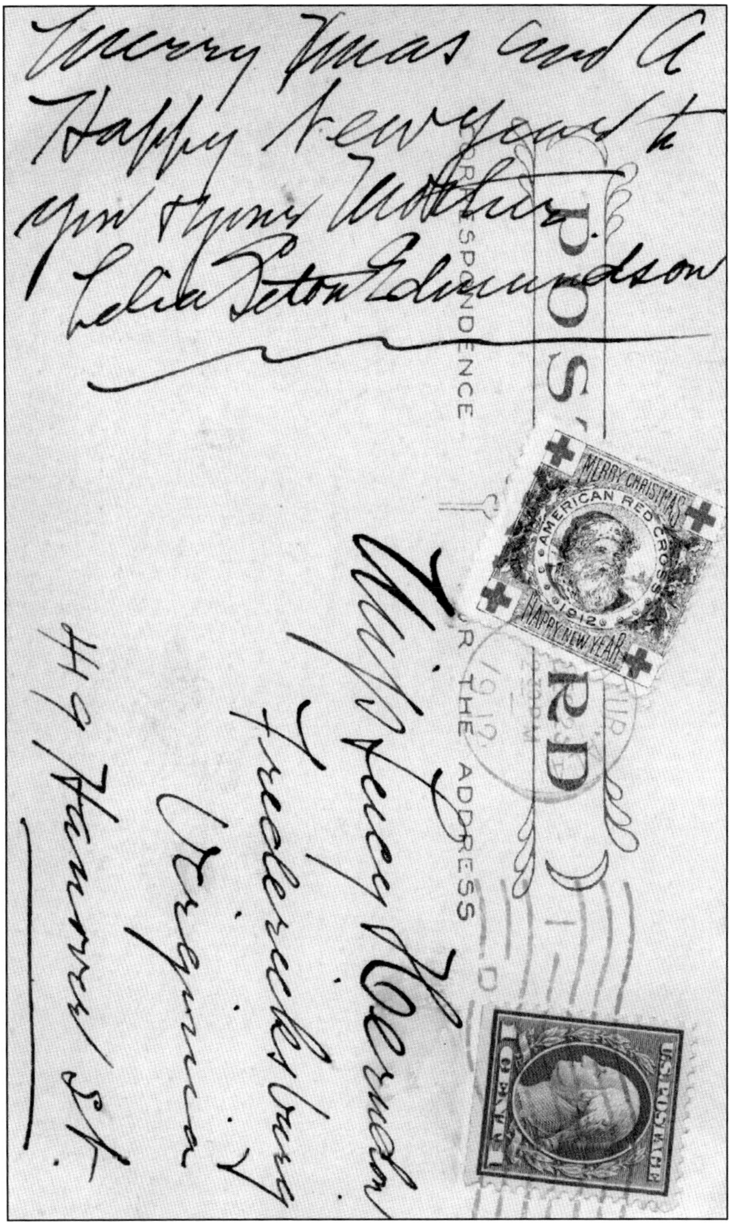

Perhaps no woman since has been beloved by the citizens of Decatur as much as Lelia Seton Edmundson, who was born in 1861 and died here in 1948 at 87 years old. She came to the city as a small child and lived in the Old State Bank. She married Charles Wilder, a Cincinnati capitalist. Wilder bought 1,700 acres in what is now Southeast Decatur. Almost two years later, Charles died, and in 1912, Lelia married Col. W.B. Edmundson. They made their home on the grand Wilder cotton plantation. She ran for Congress and championed the League of Women Voters and the TVA, even though it would flood half of her land once the dams were built. Wolverine Tube sits today on land that she sold the company. On the Fourth of July in 1936, she gave the Old State Bank to the American Legion in honor of veterans and was the largest contributor to the building fund for St. John's Episcopal Church, which still stands today. She sent this card, postmarked December 25, 1912, to Fredericksburg, Virginia.

This is the front of the card that Leila Seton Edmundson mailed in 1912, featured on the previous page. It is a real-photo postcard. Though the publisher is unknown, a stock number is barely evident just below right center. The scene is somewhere in what is today's Southeast Decatur.

A typical scene is pictured here in bringing cotton to market on the Wilder Plantation. Another real-photo postcard of unknown publication, it bears the personal stamp of Wallace Berry Edmundson on the back. After his marriage to Leila, the couple ran the plantation together and depended on the experienced laborers seen in the photograph. He died in 1938 at the age of 88.

Another real-photo postcard detailing life on the Wilder Plantation (and of unknown publication) was sent to Miss Maude Lewis in Warren, Ohio, on January 20, 1913, from nearby Hartselle. One of the most stunning photographs from the Decatur of more than a century ago, this scene played out somewhere on the southeast side of what is today's modern suburbia. Judging from the shadows, it was a sunny afternoon. A lengthy and delicately written note on the back gives an account of the day's activities. It reads, in part, "Sunday. Dear ones, This was a beautiful day. We were out walking this p.m. in woods. We sat on a log and rested while Elnora slept. The frogs are singing tonight just like spring. We are almost afraid to go back home as it is so cold up there. Look for a box by express Monday and Tuesday. We are uncomfortable with heavy clothes on. I must make new rompers for Elnora this week. Mrs. A. is real well down here. In our prayers. O.K. Love, J."

These are examples of artist Paul C. Koeber's (PCK) work with the gravure printing process, which renders soft tones, on a pair of cards. The New Decatur card at right, mailed in January 1910 to Louisville, Kentucky, was published by Dillehay & Dixon druggists of New Decatur, while the Decatur card below, mailed in 1911 to the Catskill Mountains in New York, was published by the Owl Drug Company on Bank Street. Both were printed in Germany. As seen before, each card contains previously published images to advertise the respective towns under the overall theme of the cotton boll. The New Decatur message reads in part, "Dear Cousin Edna. Received Raymond's letter and sorry you were sick. Hope you are better. It has been raining hard this morning. We had a nice Christmas and Santa brought Chas. E. a Christmas tree. He was so surprised when he got up Christmas morning and saw the tree and other things. I am not working yet but hope someday soon to get a place. Give our love to all. Your cousin, R. Riggle."

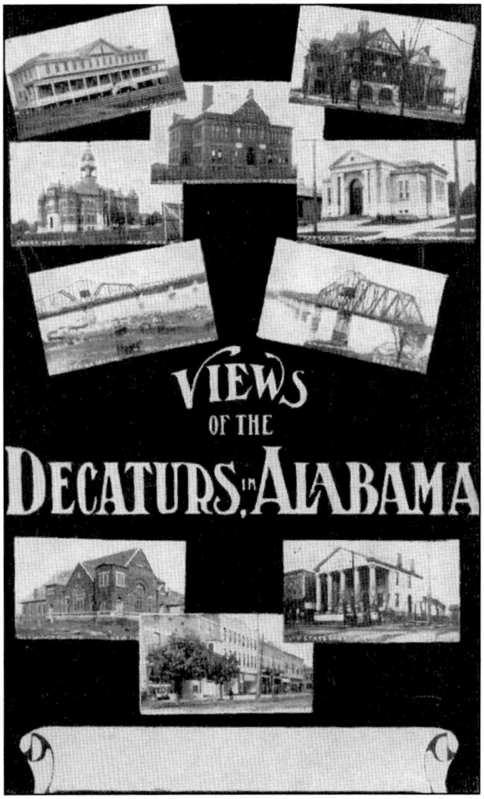

These two postcards are examples of dual-use advertisements for the two towns of Decatur and New Decatur. At left is an early undivided back card of unknown publication, but most certainly a local product. The image below is another PCK divided back card published by Dillehay & Dixon drugstore. Being a product of its time, it simultaneously advertises New Decatur and the drugstore with the message across the front reading, "New Decatur, Alabama, is a beautiful city. We have here fine streets, big high buildings, the Louisville & Nashville Railroad Shops, and just lots of pretty girls – something we all love. Meet them at Dillehay and Dixon's." Mailed in August 1909 to Mobile, Alabama, it is an example of someone needing to send a quick note. The message reads, in part, "Hello Virgil, I am up town and mama was intending to write you and didn't have time. We are all O.K. and . . . the rest are the same. Will write soon."

Five

The Railroads, Boom to Bust

Fifty-seven acres in New Decatur became home in 1889 to the Louisville & Nashville workshops, employing 1,400 men. The L&N was one part of two principal railway systems in the South, along with the Southern Railway; the latter was formed in 1894. The shops became the area's main employer for decades, with both New Decatur and Decatur dependent on the large payrolls. During World War I, railroads were federalized by the government and were not returned to private operation until March 1920. As roads got better and highways were built enabling competition from trucking companies, the L&N was trying to adapt to the new eight-hour workday and increased wages. Rail traffic slumped in 1920, and with it came pay reductions, which led to employee strikes in 1922, and for many local employees of the shops, permanent loss of their jobs. Meanwhile, railroad freight and passenger service continued to decline. When the Great Depression hit, things got worse despite occasional spurts of prosperity before then. By 1933, railroad revenues had dropped from more than $14 million to $1.7 million. Wages were cut drastically, and the L&N decided to shut down the Decatur shops.

At its height, the L&N shops employed at least 2,500. With those jobs gone, the combined town, now known as Decatur, felt the effects as more city monies were going out than coming in and residents began to leave for better opportunities elsewhere. Most of the banks were closed, and large mills subsidized with city money were sold or went bankrupt.

What is known as the golden age of postcard collecting had ended after 1914. The rise of a middle class with disposable income to spend on things like postcards, along with technical advances in photography and printing methods, had led to seven billion cards being sent through the mail worldwide in 1905. Almost a billion of those were just in the United States. These figures do not account for postcards that wound up in collections instead of a mailbox. Perhaps 50 percent of all postcards produced were collected and not mailed.

Seen above, what became Union Station, a joint station for both the L&N and the Southern Railway, was completed in 1905 at Vine and Railroad Streets. It was designed and built by the Southern Railway. Once one of the busiest transfer stations for travelers going in any direction, it sat neglected once passenger service was terminated in 1979. The building deteriorated until the city took it over and began a restoration that saved it as a museum, opening in 2017. This postcard, sent to Chillicothe, Ohio, on December 29, 1915, bears the message, "No church views obtainable here," and was sent to a collector. It is an E.C. Kropp of Milwaukee product. The view below is of the station in the 1970s before passenger service was terminated. It is a color real-photo card by Hub Gardner of Decatur for the Great American Publishing Company. Of note in the background are the old Decatur City Hall and a classic muscle car in the parking lot.

Sent on July 23, 1908, from Decatur to Ensley, Alabama, this colorized postcard was published by Owl Drug Company on Bank Street and printed in Germany for the PCK line. Labeled as "Union Passenger Station" in Decatur, the card features several people going about their business or simply leaning against the station or the passenger platforms. The card's message reads, "Hello Mollie. Why don't you write? Have been looking for a letter for a week. Goodbye. J.A.R."

A typical scene at the Union Depot in Decatur is pictured during the heyday of the steam locomotive as L&N engine No. 201 waits for passengers. In this real-photo postcard, unused and publisher unknown, none of the buildings except for the station itself still exist. No. 201 was a 4-6-2 Pacific locomotive built by the L&N in 1912. It was a K-3 class locomotive with 69-inch drivers and combined loaded weight, with tender, of 354,900 pounds. This class of locomotive was scrapped beginning in 1940, with the last disappearing in 1951.

What at first appears to be a World War I soldier in front of Decatur's Union Depot is actually a man wearing a civilian hat with a coat under his left arm. A pole leans against the building behind his right shoulder. This is a real-photo postcard, but the publisher is unknown. It was mailed June 9, 1916, to Miss Susie Kent of Gridley, Illinois. Writing on the back reads, "Dear Mother, we arrived in Decatur OK, on time and have two hours longer to [wait] . . . making five hours. John met us here. He was sure surprised. He said they never suspicioned it at all. Will write a letter soon. With love, Jack and Elmer."

Sent January 25, 1909, to Opelika, Alabama, the image on this real-photo postcard was taken where Vine Street crosses the railroad tracks by the Union Depot. At the far right, an advertisement can be seen for J.S. Alexander's Pool Hall & Bowling Alley. Most of the people on the station platform are looking directly at the photographer. Three boys listen as two men sitting on trunks and valises have a conversation in the front center right of the station. The card's sharpness and detail highlight superior German printing processes of the time.

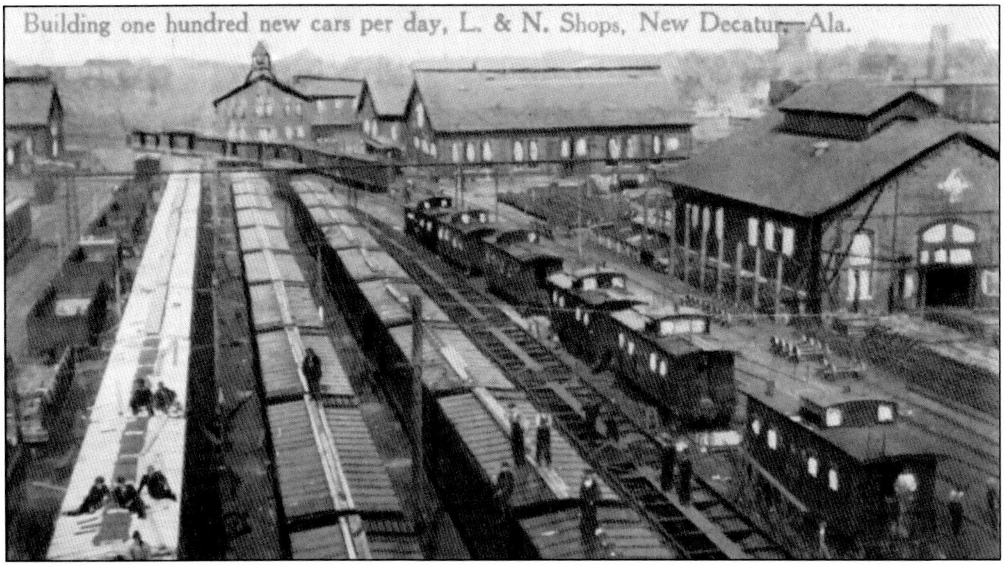

Just south of New Decatur were the L&N shops running along Fourth Avenue. Today, the area remains a railroad yard but is now in the center of the city. A heavily colorized real-photo image, the view looks north toward New Decatur with most workers stopped to gaze directly at the camera. Sent to Port Arthur, Texas, on February 28, 1914, from New Decatur, the message reads, "Dear Papa, Well we're here at last and have a good room for light housekeeping and a window for Odell. It's awful cold here now and the ground is covered with snow with more coming. Did you get my letter? Love from Grace."

This rare image shows Albany Station, referred to consistently as Grant Street Station. Built in 1888 by the L&N Railroad along First Avenue Southeast at the foot of Grant Street, the station was where president-elect Franklin D. Roosevelt addressed some 25,000 people during a 1933 pre-inaugural trip. It ceased being a full-service train depot at midnight March 31, 1929. Although tickets were no longer sold at the depot, trains continued to stop through 1936. By 1946, the station was gone, and plans were made to install a curb (farmers') market near the location; the market continues to operate there today. (Courtesy Decatur Public Library.)

Three well-dressed men with self-assured countenances pose on the running boards of Engine No. 1104 in this view looking south at the L&N yard in New Decatur. The engine is a consolidated type with a 2-8-0 wheel arrangement. More consolidateds were built than any other locomotive type. The roundhouse is to the right. Behind No. 1104 is another engine of unknown configuration. As the image was taken most probably in the warm months of the year, two of the men are wearing white hats, which was the fashion in spring and summer months. This is the only known example of this postcard and image. The publisher is unknown, and it bears hallmarks

of being a locally produced card. It was sent from New Decatur on November 19, 1912, to Elizabethtown, Kentucky. The message on the back reads, "Hello Florence, how is my dear girl this eve? Fine I hope. I did not get no letter today but I hope I will get one tomorrow. Please let me hear from you soon darling. Is [illegible] still planning on organizing Christmas? Tell her that is the bloom of the world. So good bye. Answer soon and a long letter. By By from Clyde, your ever true friend."

This Curt Teich of Chicago postcard shows the L&N shops in a view looking north with silhouettes of buildings on the horizon. Sent from New Decatur on September 21, 1908, to Hamilton, Ohio, the message reads, "We aimed to write sooner but lost your address and couldn't do it. How are you all? We are very well and hope you are same. Mrs. R. Lewis. The card is a three-color chromolithograph real-photo card. While a few of the workmen stare at the photographer, the majority, especially in the center row, continue to go about their business.

Railroad cars in the New Decatur yard are in various stages of construction in this real-photo card looking south. In the top center right, locomotive steam is rising. The only figure in the scene is one man sitting on a box between cars at center. Today's Fourth Avenue is just behind the line of trees on the left, and Central Parkway is just behind the trees on the right. Sent from New Decatur on April 18, 1908, to Paris, Tennessee, the card is a Curt Teich of Chicago product.

Next to the L&N shops on Fourth Avenue at Sixth Street Southeast were buildings that served as stores, apartments, and offices, primarily for workers and families associated with the railroad. The above card was sent from New Decatur on March 31, 1909, to Gallatin, Tennessee. A message on the back reads, "Where you see the last mark [on the front of the card] is the six buildings Willis' father owns. Where the other mark is, is where my rooms are. Have four [rooms.] Clara." This might be Clara Frohff, who is listed in the 1913 city directory as running a boardinghouse in the buildings. The below card was sent by C.H. Austin Jr. to Lynchburg, Tennessee, on July 17, 1911. He, too, marked the card as to the location of his residence as well as his father's store noted by the sign "Putnam, Austin Dry Goods" on the building's side. These buildings survived until they were demolished around 2011. Visible are a drugstore and a postal station, a mother and child watching the trolley, and several other individuals on the sidewalk. The card itself is a real-photo colorized chromolithograph printed in Germany. Its publisher is unknown.

The L&N Railroad YMCA was built in 1904 on Gordon Drive at Second Avenue and had a membership of about 900 by August 1905. One of the assets of the building was its swimming pool, and the YMCA was a popular gathering place where young men of the Christian faith could rent "small, cheerful and cleanly kept rooms, where wholesome and well-cooked meals could be served at a modest price." Sent to Miss Pearl Powell of Florence, Alabama, in September 1907, this is a real-photo postcard printed in Germany for the Souvenir Post Card Company of New York. The missive reads, "Wish U and Charles could have been with us this evening. Such a lake and river time as we did have! You better send me a word or two about Tuesday now! Because I will be back someday. Ha. Address at Arlington Hotel." At far left on the porch, six young men are engaged in conversation with a young woman. Just below them, a group of men examine a horse. The closing of the railroad shops also spelled the end of the YMCA, though the building was later used as the forerunner of Baugh-Wiley-Smith Hospital. A modern office building occupies the site today.

Unlike in the previous real-photo postcard image, all of the people in this view of the RRYMCA are focused on the photographer. Sent on August 31, 1909, to Cullman, Alabama, the message reads, "My dear sister, I will cent you a card to let you know that I got here all write and hope you are all well. So good bye to all." The card was printed in Germany and published by A.M. Simon of New York.

Sent from New Decatur on January 5, 1911, to Mrs. John B. Meyers in Hamilton, Ohio, this card is another chromolithograph by E.C. Kropp of Milwaukee. It reads, "Well, Walter was married Saturday night. What do you think of that? Mamma wants to know when your birthday is happening. All are well. R.L. Lewis." Trees had been planted on the previously bare grounds.

Another of Curt Teich's American Art series of cards, this one bears an Albany postmark for July 27, 1917. Several cards from different publishers focused on the railroad bridge across the Tennessee River. Sent to Miss Lena Lile of Leighton, Alabama, the card's message reads, "How about the camp? Are you still thinking of going? I've been so lonesome since I came home. Tell Lucille I have a cute fellow up here for her. I have already told him about Lucille and I think she will like him. Have you heard from our letter? Lovingly, Maude."

This common postcard shows "Train on Swan Lake Bridge" across from Decatur. Today, only a small section of the bridge (at far right) remains. A somewhat clumsily applied drawing of a steam locomotive pulling passenger and mail cars, it is a half-tone image of unknown manufacture. It was sent from New Decatur on August 18, 1918, to Pulaski, Tennessee. The E.C. Kropp company also produced a common image of this bridge.

Six

The Old State Bank

Soon after Decatur was chartered in 1826, the fledgling town scored a coup when it landed a branch of the Alabama state banking system in 1832. Rival claims for the bank were made by Courtland, Huntsville, Florence, and Tuscumbia. Decatur, though, was centrally located and had forceful representatives pushing for it. With the establishment of the Tuscumbia Railway and plans to expand it as the Tuscumbia, Courtland and Decatur Railroad, which would occur within a couple of years in 1834, a banking house was the cherry on top for the small town.

With the bank, Decatur was set on its path: good land for cotton, river and railroad transportation, and a state bank to finance it all. No one heeded signs of economic overexpansion, and by 1837, financial depression wreaked havoc.

Basically, if a person needed money, primarily gold or silver coin, known as "specie," he or she went to the bank and signed a note promising to pay back whatever amount was loaned plus interest. Paper money also could be redeemed for specie, and people were confident that their paper money was "as good as gold." Thomas Clark wrote in *Memorial Record of Alabama* in 1893, "Promises to pay were then the great instruments of wealth production, and the more banks the people could get, the richer they would be."

It all came crashing down when the true financial status of the state banks became known. Decatur's branch had only $1 in specie for every $100 in promissory notes. Amid the mismanagement were rumors of favoritism and collusion between bank directors and state legislators. By 1840, the Decatur branch losses were estimated at $1 million. By then, the public was aware that only a handful of people had been able to obtain loans, and of those, even fewer were responsible for the vast losses. But the damage was done. State banks, including Decatur's, lost their charters, and their assets were ordered liquidated.

The Old State Bank is one of four major buildings that survived the Civil War. Tradition states that Decatur was burned by Federal troops, but in reality, the stores, churches, and dwellings were dismantled to clear an 800-yard field of fire for artillery, and the materials were used for troop quarters within the Union army lines and breastworks that encircled the town.

Of the four buildings that remained at war's end, three—the Dancy-Polk house, the Rhea-Burleson home, and the bank—survive today. Two remain private dwellings, while the bank building is owned by the city as a museum and tourist destination. The fourth structure to survive was the McCartney Hotel on Market and Bank Streets. After the war, the hotel served as a private dwelling before being vacated. It fell into disrepair and was torn down in the early 20th century.

Above is a real-photo postcard sent from Decatur on Tuesday, March 19, 1907, to Mrs. Addie S. Greene in Rockville, Montgomery County, Maryland. It is an early undivided back card, which only has space on the reverse for an address, forcing the sender to write on the front. At the time this photograph was taken, the bank was owned by Leila Seton Wilder, who married Col. W.B. Edmundson. Next to the horse hitched in front is an advertisement for Old Sledge tobacco. Below is a real-photo postcard sent from Decatur on August 2, 1923, to Mrs. Pinkie Moon in Bellingham, Washington. The back reads, "7-31-23, Dear Mother, Just arrived here by walking eight miles this afternoon after having been 'put off.' Am on my way to Mussel Shoals to see the sights. Hope you are still having a good time. Love, Ralph." Of note in this view are the three well-dressed gentlemen chatting, one with his back to the camera. In the window next door, a lunch counter is advertised.

Published by Brown's Variety Store in Decatur, this card was mailed September 24, 1935, to Wilford, Pennsylvania. The writer makes note that alcohol wasn't available in the city and surrounding environs: "Dear folks, This is certainly a dry whiskey trip!" Alcohol was banned in the city in 1911 and didn't return, legally, until 1984. At one time, Decatur was the largest dry city in the country. The card is a chromolithograph of a real photo. The block of buildings next to the old bank was torn down in the 1970s. Notable is that the same tree appears next to the bank as in earlier photographs, but it now is encircled by grass and a sidewalk instead of mud.

This is another Curt Teich of Chicago product, published by the Anderson News Company of Florence, Alabama, and sent from Decatur on June 12, 1947, to Sheboygan, Wisconsin. The message reads, "Hi Jackie, We went to see the building on this card the other day. It's an old bank building that was the scene of some civil war battles. On some of the pillars you can see the bullet holes. Tuesday we went swimming near Wheeler Dam on the Tennessee River. The water was real clear and warm and the swimming was fun. Edith." In this image, the building has been named for the benefactor who gifted it to the American Legion. Also, the serpentine wall that flanked the bank's rear property had been added. The wall has since been removed along with the three windows in the building's front gable. That the Old State Bank survived at all during the massive urban renewal destruction of Decatur's downtown in the 1970s is nothing short of miraculous, and it now stands as a crown jewel of revitalization efforts.

Seven

Views of the Decaturs

Postcard manufacturers found a ready audience not just with the traveling public but also with officials promoting their towns for new residents and industries. A wide variety of views highlighting houses of worship, street scenes, public buildings, and even private residences were offered by publishing companies to sate the public's and collectors' appetites for postcards.

A series of tariffs in 1909 on foreign producers of postcards led to a slackening of interest. Though the tariffs were lifted in 1913, the golden years of postcard collecting were over as Europe and eventually the United States entered into uncertainty during the struggles of World War I. The market for postcards bottomed out, and many were dumped on the market at discount prices. Printing resources became difficult to obtain or were denied as they were diverted toward the war effort.

Once the First World War was over, the printing industry saw many publishers and printers go out of business as supplies were low and costs had risen. This resulted in poor quality cards, and seemingly the public's fascination with them ended.

Amendments to the Espionage Act of 1917 resulted in the Sedition Act of 1918, which covered a broad range of offenses, notably speech and expressing an opinion that cast the government or the war effort in a negative light. It forbade the use of "disloyal, profane, scurrilous, or abusive language" about the US government, its flag, or its armed forces. The act also allowed the postmaster general to refuse to deliver mail that met those somewhat arbitrary definitions. Thus, sending a postcard to a foreign country written in a foreign language could result in the sender being arrested. Local citizens' boards were formed across the country and anyone deemed insufficiently patriotic was subject to arrest. By the time the law was rescinded in December 1920, some 1,500 prosecutions were carried out resulting in more than 1,000 convictions. Sentences could range from five to twenty years in prison. Under such circumstances, it is not hard to understand that many were wary of sending a postcard with a message that could be misconstrued by anyone.

Once the war years were over and the frivolity of the 1920s picked up steam, postcard subjects generally became pretty pictures, but many also were used to express political and social agendas. The public was war-weary though, and not until the Great Depression would those latter agendas begin to be commonplace.

Postcards of the towns of Decatur and New Decatur/Albany flourished, featuring churches, street and river scenes, and notable public buildings from before World War I, between the wars, and after World War II.

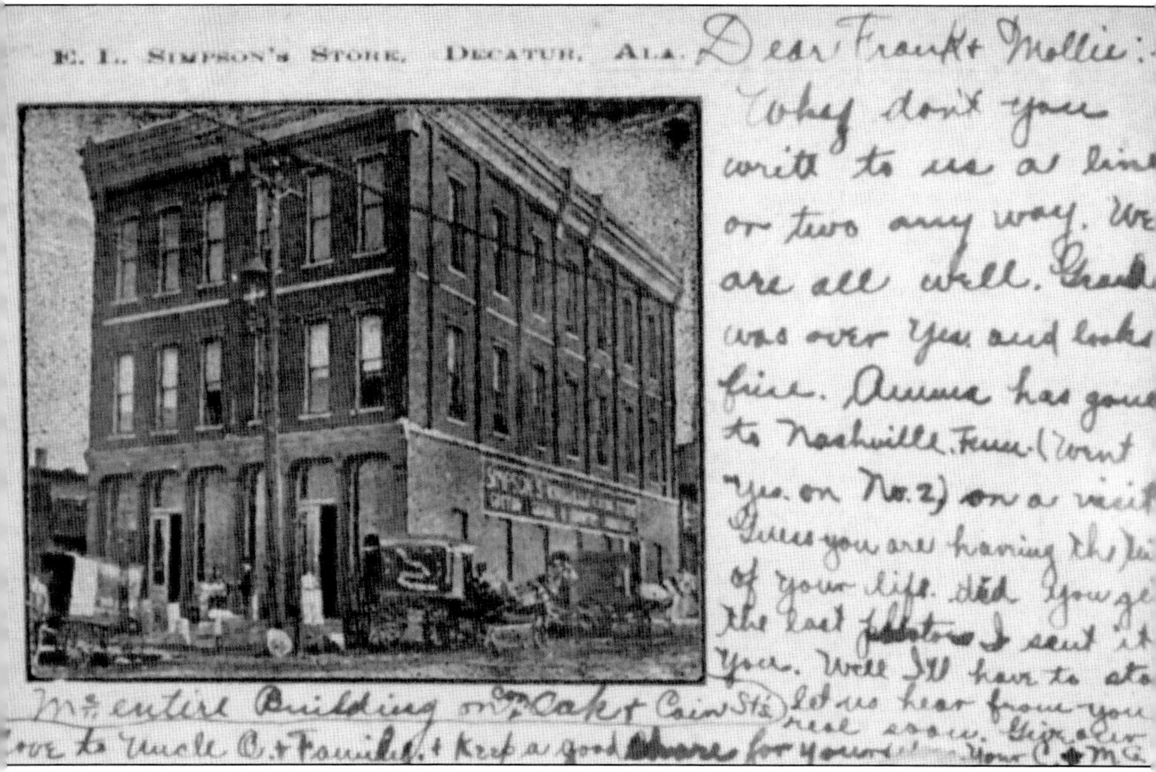

Postmarked from Decatur in September 1907 and sent to a barbershop in Springfield, Ohio, this postal card of E.L. Simpson's Store was printed using the halftone process invented by Frederick Ives in 1878. In 1887, he perfected the process, which allowed a photograph to be converted into a series of black dots so it could be affixed to a rotary press cylinder. The first halftone was used in a newspaper in 1897, and thousands of professional engravers were suddenly out of work. Simpson's Store was on the corner of Oak and Cain Streets Northeast. The building itself was constructed by Confederate veteran John T. Banks after the Civil War. In 1892, it was used as the first courthouse when the county seat was moved to Decatur, before a permanent courthouse was built. Later, the third story burned. In later years, it was used as apartment dwellings before sitting abandoned for decades. It was barely saved from the wrecking ball in the 1990s and today is an office building. An extremely rare postal card, this is the only one known to exist.

A common postcard, widely available then and now, is of Decatur's Carnegie library. Known as the "note on the door" card because of the piece of paper visible on the front door, that image shows the building in a northwesterly view. Less common is this view of the building from a southwest orientation. Mailed on May 5, 1910, from Moulton to Athens, the card carries a message that reads, "Dear Mother and Father, Without mishap I got here about sundown last evening. In spite of the sadness of my mission, my trip had many pleasant incidents connected with it – the greater of course was the visit here. Your letter will be expected Tuesday. Earl." The library building was constructed in 1904, and served as the city library for nearly 70 years. Today, it serves as the Carnegie Visual Arts Center. The card itself is another E.C. Kropp of Milwaukee product.

Two real-photo postcards show the home of Dr. Willis Edward Sterrs, called Sunny Lodge, on Washington and Vine Streets Northwest and the hospital he founded next door called the Cottage Home Infirmary and Nurse Training School. Sterrs is believed to have been the first black physician in Decatur and was one of the city's most distinguished residents. Besides founding the infirmary, which was constructed in 1900, and which may have been the city's first dedicated hospital, Sterrs owned a drugstore and a dry goods business and was widely regarded not only for his skill as a doctor but also for his eloquence as a speaker and writer on issues of the day. In the card above, Dr. Sterrs is seated just behind the automobile. His wife, Eva, is on the porch. Partially obscured by the vehicle windscreen, what appears to be a child with a doll is being cradled in his left arm. Sterrs came to Decatur in 1890, two years after receiving his medical degree, and practiced here until his death at age 53 in 1921. Eva Sterrs is remembered as fiercely devoted to improving children's educational opportunities. The home and infirmary no longer stand. The above card, postmarked onboard a Chattanooga & Memphis Railroad post car, was sent July 18, 1917, to Washington, Georgia. The below image is in the collection of the African American Museum & Library in Oakland, California.

The home of Charles Christopher Sheats stood at Ferry and Lafayette Streets behind an intricate wrought iron fence. Sheats was a schoolteacher when elected from Winston County to the Secession Convention of 1860. He opposed secession and was arrested for treason for encouraging men to join the Federal army and was also expelled from the Alabama legislature for his views. After the Civil War, he was appointed to a series of political posts during Reconstruction. He died in 1904 at age 65. His home was one of the grandest in Decatur but is thought to have succumbed to fire. Though the iron fence remains on the property, the current home was built some three decades after Sheats's death. The card itself is somewhat hard to find and was mailed in December 20, 1909, to Louisville, Kentucky. The image below, an identical card mailed May 5, 1914, to Moulton, Alabama, was sent from Thomas Marion Sheats accepting an invitation to attend graduation exercises.

This real-photo postcard of Line Street features a view from near its intersection with Cherry Street. Many of the homes pictured still stand today in the heart of the Old Decatur Historic District. Sent to Miss Marie Le Boeuf in Providence, Rhode Island, in October 1907, it is a German-printed product of the Souvenir Post Card Company of New York. An identical but colorized version of this scene was offered by the PCK company, published by the Owl Drug Company.

New Decatur's and Albany's streets were featured in postcards such as this one of Grant Street taken from near its intersection with Eighth Avenue. Today, this scene is in the Albany Historic District of Decatur. The card is a high-quality white-border chromolithograph by the E.C. Kropp Company of Milwaukee.

This card by the Kirby Studio of Decatur, published by E.C. Kropp of Milwaukee, carries a New Decatur postmark of April 14, 1916, and was sent to Montgomery, Alabama. Although the caption states it was taken on Sherman Street at Somerville Road (which is misspelled as "Somerval"), the topography and structures do not match until traveling another half block west on Sherman from that point.

Large winged griffins flanked the front and rear of the imposing Morgan County Courthouse in Decatur. Construction began in 1892 on Ferry Street at Cain Street. It burned November 12, 1926. The card itself is an E.C. Kropp product of Milwaukee, sent from Albany on October 16, 1917, to Jefferson City, Missouri. The message reads, "Hello Bill, Well I arrived here at 2 a.m. The town is the same. Tell the boys hello. The cotton and everything looks nice. Burke."

Another common view of the first permanent Morgan County Courthouse at Decatur is seen in this card, again a colorized E.C. Kropp product from a real photograph. Sent from Decatur on September 20, 1911, to Waterloo, Alabama, its message reads, "My dearest Mother, we arrived safely. Will go over to Athens about midnight. Going to the picture show tonight. Was so sorry I didn't get to tell Temple goodbye. He was so sweet to me. Will write when I get to Dec. [Decatur] Love to all, Lady." She added a postscript across the front of the card, reading, "Please write soon or sooner. Saw Mrs. Tucker at the Junction today."

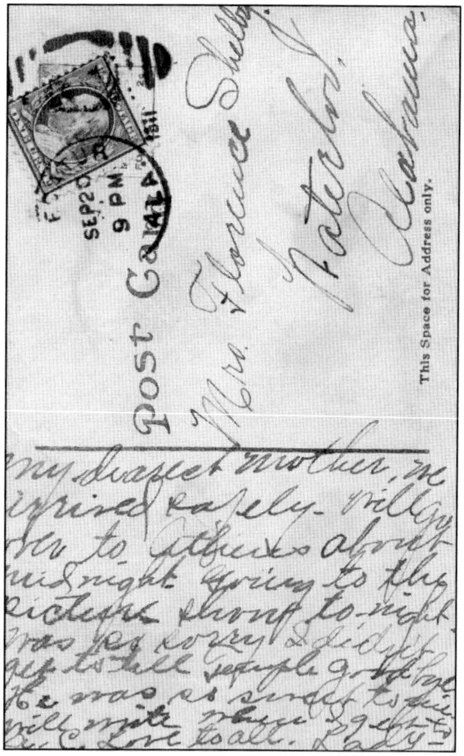

Construction on the second permanent courthouse at Decatur began in early 1928. Again located at Ferry and Cain Streets, this structure lasted until the early 1970s, when many historic buildings were razed during urban renewal efforts. It was on this courthouse that the eyes of the world focused during the second trials of the Scottsboro Boys in the 1930s. A real-photo postcard, it was published by W.M. Cline & Company of Chattanooga, Tennessee. Today, this site is a park adjacent to the front entrance of a modern courthouse.

This post office on Bank Street was the first in the nation to be designed by a black architect. Samuel Plato received the contract April 1, 1919. From this building, many postcards were sent. It served the city until a new one was built in the 1960s on Well Street. Today, the building serves as an office for a private company. The card itself is another W.M. Cline & Company product.

Standing on the corner of Bank and Vine Streets is the 1927 building for the Tennessee Valley Bank. When it opened, it touted Botticino marble fixtures, Tennessee marble floors, and American walnut woodwork. It has been the home of the Morgan County Archives since 1995. Sent to Gainesville, Georgia, on May 6, 1932, this card was postmarked onboard the Chattanooga & Memphis Railroad. It is a Curt Teich of Chicago product from the company's American Art Colored series.

Built in 1911, the Decatur City Hall at Railroad and Vine Streets served until the late 1960s, when a new seven-story city hall was constructed at Lee and Ferry Streets. The building later was torn down, and the space is a parking lot today. This card was sent from a soldier at Fort Morgan to Lawrence, Massachusetts, likely between 1942 and 1944. He wrote, "Kindly let me know if this card is OK. If not, will send you better next time. I have ordered colored cards from Wisconsin. Expect them in a few days."

Gordon School was built in 1889 on Gordon Drive in New Decatur where an abandoned fire station now sits, and consisted of a primary, grammar, and high school. The building was torn down in 1950. Of note is the building in the far right background, which still stands today and was the home of the yardmaster for the L&N railroad shops. The card is another E.C. Kropp of Milwaukee product.

Riverside High School opened after the Christmas holidays of 1923. It served as administrative offices for the school system after Decatur High School was built to replace it in 1950. Riverside was abandoned in 1973, and since then has served as retirement facilities for senior citizens. The card is a Curt Teich product by the Anderson News Company of Florence, Alabama. It was mailed from Decatur to San Diego, California, in August 1942.

Decatur High School was built fronting Prospect Drive in 1950, while the stadium behind the new school opened in time for the 1948 football season. It remains today, having just undergone a major structural change. This view of the front facade remains basically the same, although this section is now called Decatur Middle School. The linen card above is another Anderson News Company view for the Curt Teich of Chicago company. It was sent to Boscobel, Wisconsin, in January 1957. Below is a card mailed in 1929, written in German, but notable in that it too shows Riverside High School from a different angle and is labeled "Decatur" High School. This card was mailed in 1929 to Norristown, Pennsylvania. The card reflects confusion, which continues to this day, over exactly what the official name of the Riverside/Decatur High School actually was, though historical records note it as "Riverside."

Organized education in Decatur began at Lafayette and Canal Streets in 1856. After Federal troops razed the town during the Civil War, a new building was erected here. The Lafayette Street School pictured in the real-photo postcard above was built in 1904 to replace the earlier post–Civil War building. It was used for a grammar and high school until 1924, when it became a grammar school only. The structure was abandoned in 1950 and torn down. The site today is a parking lot for the First United Methodist Church, also pictured. The Lyceum Theater at Canal and Church Streets also was razed, and today its location is part of the Daiken Amphitheater. Note the muddy Canal Street with the Tennessee River in the distance. Lafayette Street cuts between the school and the church. The postcard was printed in Germany and published by the Souvenir Post Card Company of New York. It was mailed from Decatur on October 31, 1907, to West Virginia. Below is a fuller view of the school on a card mailed June 27, 1908, to Waxahatchie, Texas, It was published by the American News Company of New York and Germany.

Above is Central Baptist Church's original sanctuary at Grant Street and Fourth Avenue, completed in 1896. The education building behind the sanctuary was built in 1926. The original church building was razed for the large sanctuary seen below, which was completed in 1929. The church was named because its location was between First Baptist Church of Decatur and First Baptist Church of New Decatur. At one time it had the largest congregation in the city and in later years broadcast services on television. The card above is a chromolithograph. Below is a real-photo card published by W.M. Cline & Company of Chattanooga and shows the building around 1940. Later, the church moved to a former insurance building on US 31. The sanctuary seen below was demolished in 2016 and is an empty lot today. (Above, courtesy Decatur Public Library.)

First Presbyterian Church was first located on nearby Church Street at Bank Street in 1854. Dismantled by Federal forces during the Civil War, it filed a claim that was paid by the US government to the congregation in 1914. The congregation relocated to the location shown here at Oak and Vine Streets and built this sanctuary about 1900. It was torn down in 1953, and a new building was erected that still serves the congregation at this location today. A real-photo postcard, it is another product of W.M. Cline of Chattanooga.

This is a more modern view of First United Methodist Church at Canal and Vine Streets, which is seen in a previous card. Founded in 1834, it too fell victim to Federal troops, who dismantled it to use the materials for breastworks and soldiers' huts. The building shown on this real-photo postcard by W.B. Cline of Chattanooga was completed in 1898 and still serves the congregation today.

Westminster Presbyterian Church was organized in New Decatur in 1899 on the corner of Jackson Street at Eighth Avenue. Though there have been some structural changes, notably to the tower, the building appears basically unchanged today. The card itself is a high-quality German-printed chromolithograph and the publisher is unknown. It was sent from New Decatur on August 13, 1910, to Franklin, Kentucky, and reads, "Dear Thelman, Received your card the other day. Guess you are going to the picnic today. Will be home next Thursday. Lovingly, Rebecca."

Another W.M. Cline card, this real-photo postcard of the Grant Street Church of Christ shows the building that was erected in 1925, though the congregation traces its origins to the same spot in 1910, when meetings were held in a tent. The building, with the exception of the small structure to the right that no longer stands, remains unchanged today. The congregation announced in 2019 its intention to relocate from downtown.

Organized in Decatur around 1838, by the time of the Civil War, the congregation of First Baptist Church occupied a brick building at Lafayette and Oak Streets, which, like other churches in town, was dismantled by Federal soldiers. The building shown on this card was erected in 1908 at a cost of $25,000. This building remains virtually unchanged, but a larger sanctuary was added facing Church Street in 1971. The card appears to be an E.C. Kropp of Milwaukee product. It was sent from Moulton, Alabama, to Decatur in August 1914.

First Christian Church was built in 1897 on Moulton Street at Fourth Avenue. It was remodeled in May 1942, when the tower was completed and stone veneer applied. The congregation later moved to another location and today the building remains virtually unchanged serving other denominations. The card is another W.M. Cline of Chattanooga product.

This real-photo postcard was sent from New Decatur to Hamelin, Germany, on February 28, 1908. Constructed in 1898 on Fourth Avenue at Sherman Street by the Congregational Church, in 1901, St. Paul's Lutheran Church bought the building and called it home until 1968. In 1951, the church was turned 90 degrees and a basement added along with a new entrance and bell tower. Because of anti-German sentiment and looming espionage and sedition amendments, in 1916, sermons began being conducted primarily in English instead of German. Translated, it reads, "Miss Martha Reuter, Here you have a picture of my church. How do you like it? Back then, when this picture was taken, the vicarage was not there yet and therefore not visible here. It is right behind the schoolhouse. When is your wedding? Greetings to the Pummel, aunt, etc. Hans." The church remains today as a non-denominational congregation.

Another church turned to face a new direction is St. John's Episcopal. A result of a congregational split from St. Paul's Episcopal in Old Decatur, St. John's was built at 229 Jackson Street in New Decatur in 1893. It was rotated on August 19, 1940, to face west, with stone veneer and bell tower added later.

St. Ann's Catholic Church purchased a lot on Johnston at Fourth Avenue in Decatur in 1903, and the church building was completed in 1906 at a cost of $15,000. Here the congregation remained until moving in August 2003 to a larger facility on Spring Avenue Southwest. This building remains in its original location. A high-quality German-printed chromolithograph postcard, the card at right was sent from New Decatur on April 29, 1909, to Sheffield, Alabama. The below view is a real-photo, undivided back postcard of unknown manufacture, though the same photograph was also used by the Commercial Colortype Company of Chicago, which was in business from 1904 to 1922 and printed national view cards using a tinted halftone process. Sent from New Decatur on January 5, 1911, to Portland, Oregon, it reads, "Having seen your name in the Post Card Exchange, I thought I would send you a card. Your unknown friend, Emma Yarbrough." The house at far right across Fourth Avenue remains today.

Organized in 1898 by combing two churches then known as Southside and Eastside, Central United Methodist Church's building at Sixth Avenue at Jackson Street was first occupied in 1899. The card above shows the church before the erection of a bell tower and was sent from New Decatur to Leamington, Ontario, though the date has smudged over the years and the publisher is unknown. In the card below, sent from New Decatur in February 1912, to Bethel, Tennessee, the tower has been completed, while cows still graze in the lot across the street. To the left of the cow stood the famous Tavern Hotel. The card was published by the Commercial Colotype Company in Chicago.

As New Decatur took shape around the Central Methodist Church, landscaping and sidewalks were added as shown in this E.C. Kropp card. It was sent from New Decatur on July 1, 1914, to Cincinnati, Ohio, and references the anti-German sentiment and labor strikes then seizing the city: "Dear brother, How are you getting along? How is the . . . strike? Do you think it will do any good? And what is the reason yaw . . . not writing to some of us? All you sick or is something wrong? Please write at once. Brother Beau." Below is another real-photo card from the Cline Company of Chattanooga and shows the church in the 1940s.

Several versions exist of this card. Some are real-photo postcards and some monotone colorizations as well as chromolithographs of the same image. Examples sent through the mail from Decatur or New Decatur vary, with postal dates from 1907 through 1916. The earliest, a real-photo card, was sent from Decatur on May 6, 1907, to Birmingham, Alabama, to Miss Velma Graves. Because postal regulations prohibited anything on the back except for addresses only, senders were forced to write on the white lower border or across the front, as seen in this example: "Hello Velma, In Decatur today. Hope to see you some Sunday soon. Will write you soon. A.B." The publisher is unknown, and it bears the hallmark of being a locally-produced image. Known among some locals as "Resurrection Island," because it was popular for baptisms, the location today is part of Brickyard Landing Condominiums. Due to construction of dams by the Tennessee Valley Authority, the water at this location is more than 30 feet deep today.

Travelers often sent postcards home depicting pastoral scenes, and several of the Decatur area were available, usually focusing on Flint Creek, Swan Creek, or the Tennessee River. This card of Swan Lake was sent from Decatur on February 1913, to Miss Clara Elliott of Bedford, Virginia. It reads, "Hello! How are you by now? Fine I hope. The train was eight-hours late and I did not get here until 10 O'clock and have got about eighty miles to go yet. When is Nick going to leave his party? I sure would like to come Monday Feb. 10th. By by Oscar." The card is a hand-colored real-photo. Publisher is unknown.

Another real-photo postcard that often was hand-tinted or reproduced with added extra color, and is quite common to find, is this one showing two people in a small rowboat on Flint Creek. The actual location is most likely a small bridge on today's Harris Station Road near the pistol and rifle range in Tanner, Alabama.

If this image looks familiar, it is because it is the same one used for a heavily colorized card titled "Moonlight on the Tennessee River, New Decatur, Alabama," which appears on the back cover. A real-photo postcard, this is the base image used by the unknown artist who inserted a rowboat, moon, and dark-colored tints to create the fanciful image for that card. The actual location is believed to be near today's walking trail at Point Mallard Park, which once was part of the Wilder Plantation. The publisher is unknown.

One of the most common Decatur postcards is this one showing 10 men and a dog called "View of Logging Camp in Morgan Co." A real-photo postcard and the basis for various colorized versions of the same scene, it is a PCK product published by Pride & Mason of Decatur and printed in Germany. Sent from Decatur on October 9, 1909, to Jackson, Ohio, the writer noted, "Plenty of big trees down here." The men's faces, all with stern and resigned countenances, some possibly war veterans, show the hard life of logging old-growth hardwoods in the area. Where in Decatur or Morgan County this scene took place is unknown.

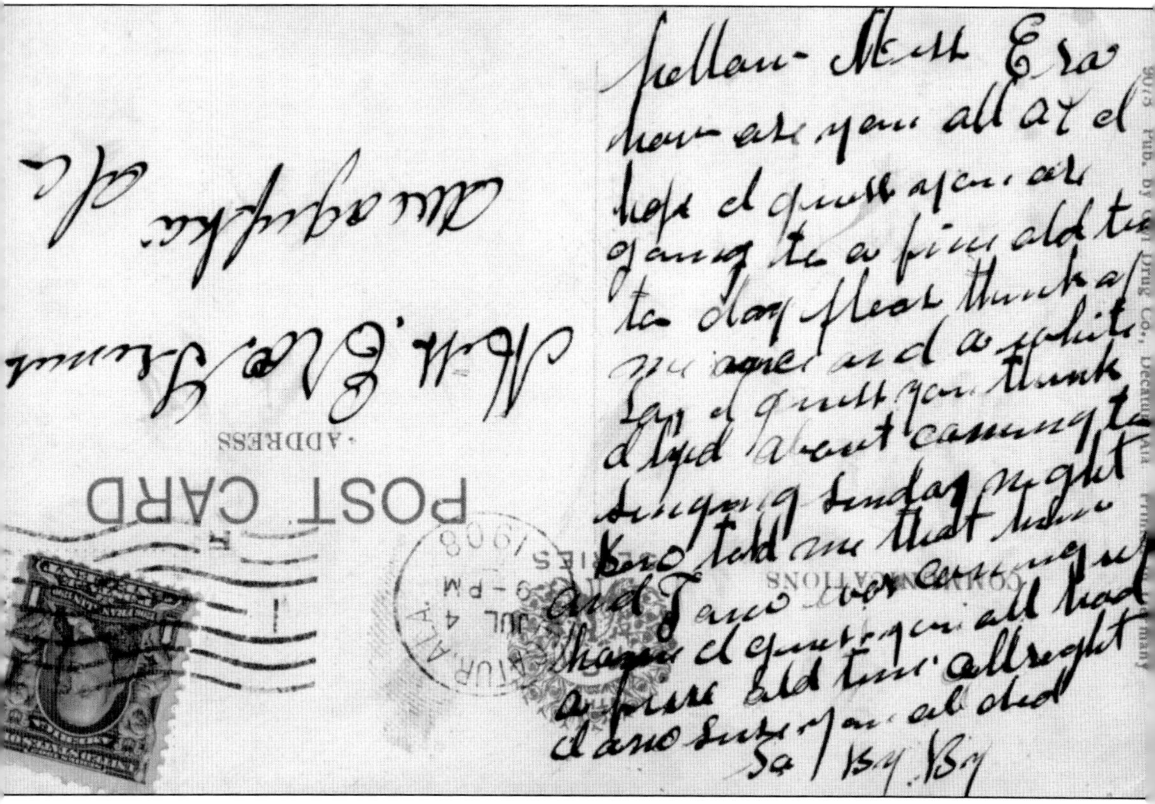

This is the back of a card mailed July 4, 1908, from Decatur, with the same logging scene as seen on the previous page. It also is a PCK product but was published by the Owl Drug Company in Decatur. It was sent to Weogufka, Alabama, which was settled in 1836 by a migration of 40 Cherokee Indians and mixed-white and Indian families who fled the infamous Trail of Tears. Listed as an incorporated community in the 1920 census, Weogufka didn't appear again on a census until 2010, with a population of 282. Written partially in dialect, it reads in part, "Hello Miss Era, how are you all? OK I hope. I guess you are going to a fine old time today."

The American Oak Leather Extract Company in Decatur was founded in 1887, and operated here until the late 1940s. It manufactured an extract used in tanning. Among the company's pursuits was shipbuilding. Shown in this postcard is a portion of the shipyard downstream from the landing near the railroad bridge shown in an earlier chapter. The *Decatur No. 1* steamboat was built by the company in 1900. By 1910, Decatur had the only boatyard between Chattanooga and Paducah, Kentucky, where boats were built and repaired. This boat was one of the last to be operated off Decatur through the 1930s, when costly hull repairs doomed it to the scrap yard. The card is unsent, publisher unknown, and is quite common. This area of the river later became part of the Ingall's Iron Works shipyard. Though the area today is submerged, a heritage of shipbuilding lives on at the site, which is now Ingall's Harbor and Pavilion, a boat launch and entertainment facility.

Begun as Connecticut Mills at the end of Nineteenth Avenue Southeast in 1927, this card shows the plant after it was taken over by Goodyear in 1933. With 200,000 square feet of space and 32,000 spindles, it produced more than seven million pounds of cord and automobile fabrics per year at that time. Being in the center of the Cotton Belt and with good water and rail transportation, raw materials could be obtained at minimal cost, making Decatur an attractive location. The plant remains today, with little outside structural change, under foreign ownership. Published by Curt Teich of Chicago, the card was mailed from Decatur in July 1943 to Louisville, Kentucky, describing a bus trip: "Hello. Now it's 6:20 a.m. Sunday morn. Had a very nice trip so far. Same seat all the way. Will soon be in Birmingham [and] this will change. Slept fairly well and feel fine. Rather warm down this way. How [is] little Fat Alan? Tell him to stop growing till I get home. Lots of babies on the bus, little ones too. Mother."

Cooper-Wells Hosiery Mills was located on Second Avenue at Gordon Drive. Built in 1927, the company is credited with helping the city weather the Great Depression with good-paying jobs for its residents. The plant made full-fashioned women's hose with a seam down the back. Once nylon and seamless hose caught on, the seamed products fell out of favor. The company closed its doors in 1954. During World War II, production was diverted to manufacturing aprons, mattress covers, and cotton hose for the Women's Army Corps. After closing, the building housed a building supply store, which later burned. The site today is a landscaped parking lot for Morgan County Area Transportation System (MCATS). Mailed on May 25, 1939, the card is a Curt Teich American Art Colored product and reads, "Be at home next Wednesday. Having a good time."

The Alabama Hosiery Mill was on Eleventh Street at Sixth Avenue Southeast. Like Cooper-Wells, it provided good-paying jobs, and both businesses had organized baseball, softball, bowling, and basketball teams and a healthy rivalry between them and other local industries. After the mill closed and abandoned the building in 1955, it became part of Decatur Shopping Center in 1962, housing a W.T. Grant department store, which had vacated its downtown location. The building remains today, housing a furniture store. The old windows from its days as a mill, bricked up now, are still plainly visible from Eleventh Street. Another Curt Teich American Art series postcard, it was mailed from Decatur on July 24, 1948, to Wauwatosa, Wisconsin. It reads, "Suppose you're almost ready to leave on your trip. Wish I had your new sun back dress here. Think I need it more than you do. Had a nice trip down in air conditioned train and seat reserved. Had four hours wait at Nashville so took a ride to see the nice homes. Probably back last week of August. Eva."

Postcards showcasing local businesses and buildings continued as a viable marketing tool into the 1960s and 1970s, as the next few cards attest. The First National Bank of Decatur was located on East Moulton Street at Fourth Avenue. Advertised as a "new ultra-modern banking center," the building remains today little changed, last occupied by a Wells Fargo branch. The card itself was published by Koppel Color Cards of New Jersey, which specialized in photochrome color postcards in the 1960s.

Another Koppel Color Card was published showing the Decatur Chamber of Commerce in the mid-1960s. The building on Sixth Avenue is unchanged and still in use today by the chamber. Of note is that the card was sent from Hammond, Indiana, in 1969, most likely as a contest entry by a 12-year-old girl to *Bozo Circus*, a popular children's program that premiered on WGN-TV Chicago in 1961, broadcasting every weekday at noon.

Generic postcards always have been available and appealed to travelers inclined to convey certain emotions to the folks back home. The card above, published by Plastichrome Colourpicture Publishers of Boston, Massachusetts, was sent from Decatur in August 1959 to Flint, Michigan. It features a generic real color photograph. The card reads, "Hi Aunt Sue. Boy you sure are missing it down here. We took a big hike yesterday when we visited some people in the mountains. The scenery is just plain beautiful. See you soon. Take care of yourself and granny too. Love, Jo." Below is an image used in the early 20th century with some publishers taking liberty to have a staff artist paint a train into the scene to appeal to as many people as possible. It is an E.C. Kropp product.

These two cards with the notation "Color by Hub Gardner" and published by Chromolithic Cards of Decatur for the Alabama Mountain Lakes tourism bureau feature the Wave Pool at Point Mallard Park. Built in the early 1970s, it was the first wave-activated pool in the southeastern United States and still operates today. Above is a card mailed August 18, 1977, to Laguna Hills, California, with the writer noting, "I am doing a little fishing [and] the weather is fine." Below is an overview of the aquatic center at the park, a Decatur postmark clearly evident on the front. Sent in July 1976 to Ashland, Ohio, it reads, "Hi! I had to send you a card so you could see where we are. It is really a great place for kids to vacation. The 4th of July celebration was yesterday the 3rd. It was great. We even saw the Miss Alabama contest. It has rained everyday but one."

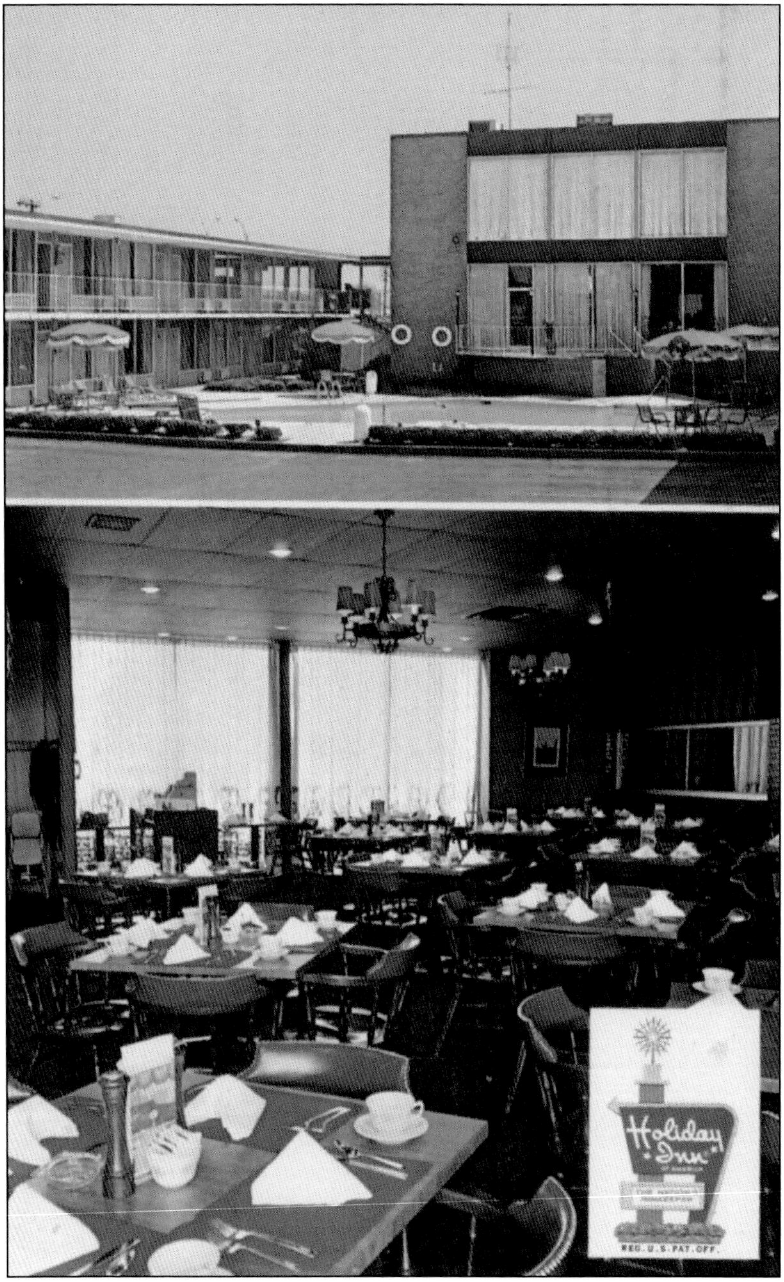

Holiday Inn called a location next to Keller Memorial Bridge and the Tennessee River home for more than 20 years beginning in the late 1950s. A Doubletree by Hilton operates there today. This card is one of two sent from that location. Mailed in March 1966 to Muskegon, Michigan, it reads, "Hiya Ruth Anne. We are in this town of Decatur, Alabama having a good time. It's going to be in the 60s tomorrow. Grandpa." A card sent from here in March 1969 to Charleston, West Virginia, was not as complimentary: "Sunday p.m. OK worry wart, relax! We made it here our first night. It was too early to stop in Nashville – only 3 pm. Had snow in Lexington, Ky. Windy and cold here, but good interstate most of the way. Just had a lousy meal and ready for bed. One hour earlier here so will get extra sleep before tomorrow's journey. Dickie and Charlie."

A color postcard manufactured by the Scenic South Card Company of Bessemer, Alabama, for Koppel Color Cards of Hawthorne, New Jersey, a major publisher and printer of photochrome postcards in the 1960s, is this one titled Haunted Castle. Recognizable to many area residents as the once grand home of Col. James Saunders called Rocky Hill, the house stood some 18 miles west of Decatur. Built in 1858, the residence had a colorful history and was the subject of numerous ghost stories. After the last of Saunders's descendants abandoned the home in 1926, it stood vacant until Gordon McBride of Decatur bought it in 1961 and demolished it the following year. McBride built a modern home out of the materials on Meadowbrook Road Southeast in Decatur, which still stands today. The card's view of Rocky Hill actually is of the front of the home, which faced the railroad running between Decatur and Tuscumbia. Today, a modern home sits at the location in Lawrence County, and only the two cedar trees appearing in this view still stand, flanking the modern home's backyard swimming pool.

Somerville, Alabama, was the first county seat, before Decatur was selected. And though accusations of voter fraud were tossed around, the county seat has remained in Decatur since 1892. This is a Koppel Color Card for the Alabama Post Card Company of Bessemer. The description mislabels the statue of Lady Justice as a "miniature Statue of Liberty." Although the building was a victim of urban renewal and no longer remains, the columns are featured today on a private home in the area. Both the Confederate war memorial and Lady Justice statues remain in place in what is now called Cotaco Park, named after Morgan County's first moniker.

Another typical card promoting Decatur as "the fresh water fishing capital" is from the late 1960s–early 1970s and was published by the Alabama Post Card Company of Bessemer, Alabama, with "Kolor by Kent." The card promotes the location near Keller Memorial Bridge in the background as a place "where thousands of people come to enjoy water sports every week." Though the card was unsent, a note on the back reads, "This is it while it is pretty. It's ugly now with the flood waters."

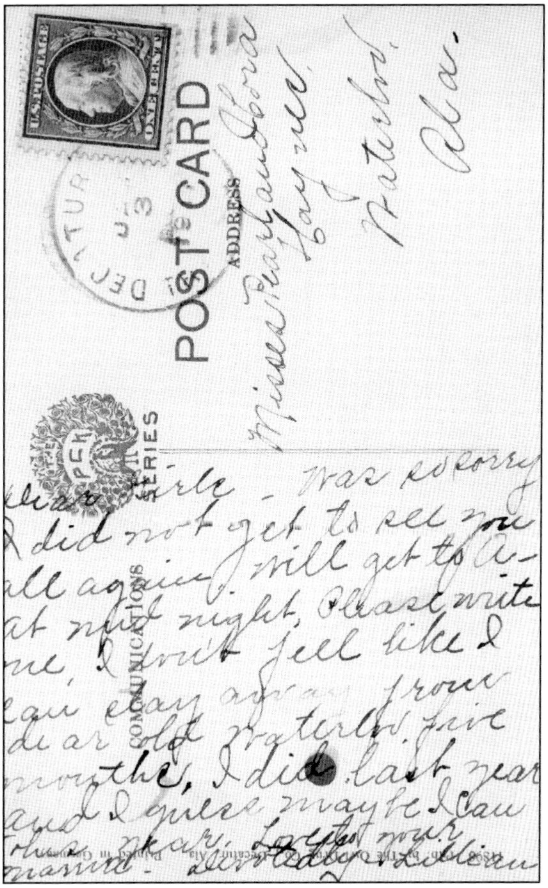

Once a novel and low-cost way to communicate, postcards featuring Decatur became part of a collecting craze, a valuable marketing tool, and wound up inadvertently documenting various aspects of a city's and a people's history. As this final card, sent from Decatur to Waterloo, Alabama, in 1912, says "Dear girly . . . Was sorry I did not get to see you all again. Please write me."

Consistent with our mission to preserve history on a local level, this book was printed in South Carolina on American-made paper and manufactured entirely in the United States. Products carrying the accredited Forest Stewardship Council (FSC) label are printed on 100 percent FSC-certified paper.